Lake Okeechobee

Area

Bill & Carol Gregware

*To The Goshen Library
Enjoy the Real Florida!
Bill Gregware
3/8/09*

 Pineapple Press, Inc.
Sarasota, Florida

Inquiries should be addressed to:
Pineapple Press, Inc.
P.O. Box 3899
Sarasota, Florida 34230

LIBRARY OF CONGRESS CATALOGING-IN-PUBLICATION DATA

Gregware, Bill, 1931-
        Guide to the Lake Okeechobee area / by Bill and Carol Gregware. — 1st ed.
                p.   cm.
        Includes bibliographical references and index.
        ISBN 1-56164-129-4 (alk. paper)
        1. Okeechobee, Lake, Region (Fla.)—Guidebooks.
I. Gregware, Carol, 1935-   .   II. Title.
F317.04G74   1997
917.59'390463—dc21   96-37652
                                              CIP

First Edition
10 9 8 7 6 5 4 3 2 1

Design by Carol Tornatore
Printed and bound by McNaughton & Gunn, Saline, Michigan

Contents

Acknowledgments

For their support of this project special thanks are due Diane Kinchen, executive director of the Okeechobee Tourist Council, and Chuck Freed, member of the Okeechobee Tourist Council and owner of the Zachary Taylor RV Resort. Also, to Barry Lege, Audubon Warden at Lake Okeechobee, and Mary Gentry, naturalist and nature writer from Largo, Florida, for their review of the flora and fauna sections. Betty Williamson, fifth-generation Floridian and president of the Okeechobee Historical Society, reviewed the history section, and Doctor Blair Snoke of Seminole, Florida, an avid bass fisherman who fishes Lake Okeechobee at every opportunity, reviewed the fishing section. Thanks also to numerous other Okeechobeelanders who contributed their knowledge of the area.

The help of those who contributed their knowledge of the Okeechobee area is highly appreciated. However, responsibility for any errors that may be contained in this guidebook rests solely with the authors.

Introduction

What, Where, When, Why, and How?

What is it?

Lake Okeechobee is a huge freshwater lake. The word "Okeechobee" means "big water" in the Seminole Indian language. Indeed, Lake Okeechobee is big, covering about 730 square miles, or 470,000 acres. It's so large that local folks like to brag about it.

The U.S. Army Corps of Engineers, an organization with a lot to say about what goes on around the mighty lake, claims it's the "largest of Florida lakes and second largest fresh water lake in the United States." A popular computer software encyclopedia states it is "the third largest freshwater lake within the confines of the United States." A nice salesperson at Wal-Mart in Okeechobee proudly states that it's "the second biggest lake within the confines of the United States."

Actually, they're all a bit wrong. The correct way to say it is: Lake Okeechobee is the second largest freshwater lake wholly within the confines of the United States. Here's why it needs to be said precisely this way: All of the five Great Lakes are larger than Lake Okeechobee, but only one, Lake Michigan, lies wholly within the confines of the United States. The other Great Lakes are half in Canadian waters. Okeechobee is the third largest lake totally within the United States, but the second largest, Great Salt Lake, is, of course, a saltwater lake.

Where is it?

Lake Okeechobee is in the interior of subtropical southern Florida, just north of the Everglades. Its waters lie within thirty miles of the Atlantic Ocean, the Florida shores of which were some of the first New World lands discovered by Europeans. The state itself was the first frontier in North America. Surprisingly, the mighty lake was virtually unseen by Europeans until centuries later. Actual settlement of the area around the inland sea did not occur until near the beginning of the twentieth century. Long after the American West was tamed, this area remained wild and primitive. Consequently, Lake Okeechobee and the adjoining Everglades are often referred to as the last frontier.

Lake Okeechobee has been called the mother of the Everglades because, historically, overflow from its southern shore spilled life-giving waters into the Glades. But nature's grand scheme of water drainage in southern Florida has been replaced by a human plan that includes a myriad of dredged streams, canals, locks, and floodgates.

Sometimes the word "Okeechobee" is confused with "Okefenokee." The latter, however, is a large swamp located (partly) in Florida but far to the north of Lake Okeechobee, along the Florida/Georgia boundary.

Why go there?

If one is looking for an idyllic place to relax for a few days and do a little fishing, hunting, or birdwatching and nature study, the Lake Okeechobee area is a good choice. It is also a pleasant place to spend winters or to live permanently. The area is unpretentious with a clean, neat setting and no exasperating crowds. Traffic is reasonable, the crime rate is low, housing is inexpensive, and there are lots of friendly folks. And it's in a natural wonderland full of intriguing flora and fauna with an enormous lake in the middle. There's no salt spray here to rust a car or other metallic devices. Yet, it's within an hour's drive to beautiful sand beaches on the Atlantic Ocean and not much farther from the Gulf of Mexico shores. From Lake Okeechobee, it is an easy trip to all the other attractions of southern Florida. The immense lake is world-famous for fine fishing, but those who don't fish can find other enticing activities and things to explore.

For Florida visitors who have tired of expensive theme parks and exotic zoos, the Lake Okeechobee area provides a rewarding alternative — a place to see the real Florida. As one wag put it, "If Disney owned Lake Okeechobee, they'd put a fence around it and charge an exorbitant fee to enter. Tourists would flock here, saying it was one of the greatest things they'd ever seen!" Fortunately, for nature lovers and others, there's no charge to visit this wonderland.

Lake Okeechobee is, in a word, incredible. Where in the United States can one find such an enormous, beautiful body of water without houses jammed around its shores? As outrageously priced as waterfront property is today, the shore of Lake Okeechobee should be a mecca for developers and real estate salespersons. Despite all the water and over 130 miles of shoreline, there are no private houses on the waterfront. A huge wall, the massive thirty-four-foot-high Herbert Hoover Dike, has been built entirely around the lake. The few properties located on the immediate waterfront include four campground/marinas, one each on the north, east, south, and west shores, and an RV resort on the north shore.

A young lady who manages a restaurant on the north side of the lake says, "I get people in here all the time who say they've been driving for miles and haven't seen the lake yet. 'Where in the world is it?' they ask me. I have to tell them it's on the other side of that big wall over there!"

The Lake Okeechobee area seen today has been profoundly affected by artificially confining the leviathan lake. Why has a unique barrier to waterfront development been constructed around one of Florida's greatest natural wonders? A look at the origin and history of this splendid lake is necessary to understand what is now found here, in the liquid heart of Florida. Several chapters of this book will focus on the events that gave rise to today's Okeechobeeland.

When is the best time to visit?

Some area enthusiasts would say that it is always a good time to visit the Lake Okeechobee region. In truth, most visitors come in the cooler months of fall, winter, and spring when the heat and insects are less of a problem. On the other hand, the hotter months are less crowded. There are residents who live and work here year round. Life goes on in the hot months and local folks go about their daily routines of working, mowing the yard, shopping, etc. Fishing the great lake in the morning hours can be very pleasant even in the hottest part of summer. Of course, being able to retreat to the comfort of an air-conditioned car or house provides relief. Another benefit to visiting in the summer months is that they are the off season, so lodging is cheaper. The most popular visitor's season is generally regarded as December 1 to May 1.

For those who visit in the winter months, it is wise to bring some light cold-weather clothing. The temperature rarely falls to near or below freezing, but it can and sometimes does.

How does one get there?

Most visitors arrive by private automobile. From the north the quickest ingress is to travel south on the Florida Turnpike to Ft. Pierce and then west to Okeechobee on Route 70. Or, one can exit the Florida Turnpike near Yeehaw Junction (yes, there is such a place!) and take U.S. 441 south to Okeechobee. This route provides an interesting drive through Okeechobee County and the heart of Florida's dairy land. To reach the area from the south, drive the seventy-some miles up Route 27 from Miami to South Bay on the southern shore of Lake Okeechobee. From the east, it's an easy forty-mile drive on

U.S. 441 from West Palm Beach to Belle Glade, located on the eastern shore of the lake. Coming from the west, the Florida Cracker Trail (Route 64) makes an interesting drive, as does Route 70 through Arcadia or Route 809 from Ft. Myers.

Amtrak is still another way to reach the Lake Okeechobee area. There is a station at Okeechobee, about four miles from the lakefront. Arriving from the north and the Orlando (Disney World) depot, Amtrak stops at Kissimmee, Winter Haven, Sebring, and then Okeechobee. From the south, Amtrak stops at Miami, Hollywood, Ft. Lauderdale, Deerfield, Delray Beach, West Palm Beach, and then Okeechobee.

Some people visit Lake Okeechobee by boat. If a boat is less than 250 feet long with a beam under 50 feet and draws no more than 8 feet of water, it can be navigated into Lake Okeechobee from either the Atlantic Ocean side on the east or the Gulf of Mexico side on the west along the Cross Florida/Okeechobee Waterway. Watercraft — from boats and barges of the maximum size to small kayaks and canoes — can enter Lake Okeechobee by this waterway. Beginning at Stuart on the Atlantic Ocean, a boat can travel the St. Lucie Canal to Lake Okeechobee. From Fort Myers on the Gulf of Mexico, the route goes up the Caloosahatchee River into Lake Okeechobee. Both directions require passing through locks to enter the lake itself. Most visitors arrive in privately owned boats, but there are a few commercial boats that can sometimes be taken into the area. For example, one boat now operating allows a visitor to board in Long Island, New York, and debark several days later in Pahokee on the east shore of Lake Okeechobee.

Many of the towns around Lake Okeechobee have airports that will accommodate small aircraft. Some local chambers of commerce will pick up visitors flying into their airports and take them to their lodging.

The Palm Tran is a bus service from West Palm Beach to Belle Glade, South Bay, Pahokee, Canal Point, and other localities along the east and south areas of Lake Okeechobee. Greyhound provides bus service to some of the lake towns.

For the hardiest of travelers, the soon-to-be completed Florida National Scenic Trail will provide a path for hikers and mountain bikers to enter the lake area, from either the north or the south. Once at Lake Okeechobee, the Scenic Trail follows the top of the Herbert Hoover Dike for 110 miles around the lake. The trail on top of the dike allows a great panoramic view of this natural wonderland (See the Hiking/Biking Tour).

However a visitor arrives, whenever during the year, and for whatever purpose, it's a good idea to check with the local chamber of commerce for scheduled events and to get the latest recommendations for lodging, dining spots, and other information. Restaurants, inns, and other attractions can close suddenly, so it's always best to obtain an update from local informational sources.

Following are phone numbers for the chambers of commerce of the principal towns around Lake Okeechobee:

Okeechobee: (941) 763-6464 or (800) 871-4403

Indiantown: (407) 597-2184

Pahokee: (407) 924-5579

Belle Glade: (407) 996-2745

Clewiston: (941) 983-7979

Moore Haven: (941) 946-0440

Part 1 THE PAST

1   Roots

*O*nce, the land now named Florida was part of another continent, united with an area called Morocco. Awesome earthquakes rumbled and huge faults cracked the ground. A newly formed basin separated Florida from Morocco and the sea poured into this low area. Volcanoes under the water spewed lava. Newly erupted material forced its way between the original neighboring land masses and began to push them apart. Slowly, almost imperceptibly, the masses separated, riding on underlying molten rock.

For eons, the land drifted beneath an ancient sea and inched its way westward, as it still does today. As the millennia passed, the shells of countless dead sea creatures rained down upon the submerged land, slowly building up thousands of feet of limestone sediments.

At times during the Great Ice Ages, the seas shrank because much of the Earth's water became frozen in gigantic glaciers which covered a large part of the northern regions. Sea level fell by hundreds of feet, and the submerged land was exposed to air. Florida became a huge, broad peninsula over two hundred miles wide in places.

Animals overran the land. Huge woolly mammoths, mastodons, massive ground sloths, saber-toothed tigers, bears, wolves, rhinoceroses, horses, llamas, bison, camels, giant armadillos, and other strange creatures roamed the grassy terrain.

When the glaciers melted (as they did several times during the Ice Age), sea level rose to cover much of the land, and the

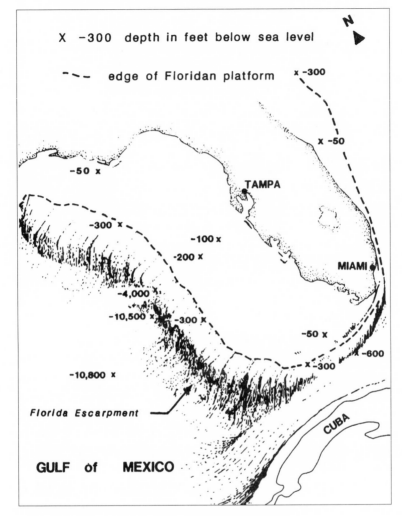

X −300 depth in feet below sea level

N

−~~ edge of Floridan platform   x -300

x -50

-50 x

TAMPA

-300 x

-100 x

-200 x

MIAMI

-4,000

-10,500 x   -300 x

-50 x

-10,800 x   -300   x -600

Florida Escarpment

CUBA

GULF of MEXICO

OBLIQUE VIEW OF THE FLORIDA PLATEAU   During the Ice Ages, when sea level dropped by as much as 300 feet, a vast land area on the Florida Platform was exposed, reaching over 100 miles west of Tampa. Land animals lived across the huge peninsula at this time.

Florida Geological Survey, Special Publication 35, 1994

animals retreated to the north where it was higher and drier. The last time massive continental glaciers formed and sea level dropped sharply, a new creature appeared on the grassy plains.

Each time sea level fell during the Ice Ages, streams and rivers flowing off the new land in their quest for the shortest and easiest way to the sea worked their way into the cracks and crevices of the underlying soft limestone. In places, large underground conduits were carved out of the bedrock. As sea level became progressively lower and many streams changed their courses, some of the higher water passageways were abandoned and became dry caves and caverns. These were water-filled again when sea level rose once more.

In times of widespread continental glaciation, low sea level, and dry caves, animals sought shelter in some of these subterranean cavities. During the last low sea level period (about ten to fifteen thousand years ago) the new creature began to use the caves.

Scientists tell us that *Homo sapiens* first entered the Americas via a land bridge across the Bering Strait. Apparently, some of these new arrivals soon retired from the frigid north and migrated to Florida. Indications are that right after the first wave of migration over the Bering Straits, humans almost immediately showed up in sunny Florida — sunny, at least in the summers, but not humid. Florida was then a relatively arid place where water was scarce, occurring only in a few streams, at the bottom of old sinkholes, and at springs. There was no Lake Okeechobee at that time. Florida was largely a grassy, flat area, probably resembling parts of the southwestern Great Plains today. Herds of enormous animals grazed these Florida plains.

The stage was set, however, for the birth of what would become Lake Okeechobee. Bedrock had formed a spoon-shaped concavity in the center of the peninsula and the low area was later named the Okeechobee Depression by geologists. This concavity, combined with rock and sand ridge high areas on either side, created a funneling effect. Rainfall from the central part of the Florida Peninsula formed streams that flowed south and eventually ponded at Lake Okeechobee.

This unusual drainage system persists today. Instead of runoff in southern Florida flowing for the shortest distance to sea level, it runs down to the end of the peninsula. Rainfall from as far north as the Orlando area flows south toward Lake Kissimmee and, from there, into the Kissimmee River, which empties into Lake Okeechobee. In the past, when the lake overflowed, distributaries along its southern shores discharged the life-giving water into the Everglades, which ultimately drained its excess waters into Florida Bay.

Around and under most of Lake Okeechobee, the bedrock is a hundred-thousand-year-old limestone called the Fort Thompson Formation, which overlies an older formation named the Caloosahatchee Marl (about two million years old). Both of these formations are generally light gray to white marine rocks literally full of beautiful, well-preserved fossil shells.

The actual birth of Lake Okeechobee begins with the ending of the last Ice Age. The massive continental glaciers that covered so much of northern North America began to melt. Thawing was not completed overnight because the mighty glaciers covered sites such as present-day Detroit with ice over a mile deep. The weight of this frozen water was so ponderous that it depressed the surface of the Earth.

Melting ice caused the sea level to rise once more and the area of exposed land was decreased. At times during the past ten to fifteen thousand years, sea level rose a foot or more per year, a relatively rapid rate. Conditions stabilized about five thousand years ago, leaving the terrain looking much as it does today.

As the climate warmed, fresh water became abundant on the new and smaller peninsula. It became an ideal place to live for both human and beast. However, something curious

FOSSIL COLLECTING

The Lake Okeechobee area is a productive spot to collect marine fossils. There are abundant clams, snails, sea urchins, sand dollars, worm tubes, and other relics of the ancient ocean scattered around the lake area. Although natural outcrops of exposed bedrock are rare in southern Florida, the numerous excavations for canals and other construction have left fossil-rich debris nearly everywhere. Many of the species are identical to those found in the ocean today but their original colors have faded to gray or white. Some collectors attempt to restore their natural colors by painting them. The hobby of collecting Florida fossils is not only fascinating, but it does no harm to the ecosystem as does the now largely illegal collecting of live specimens. One should be careful, however, where fossils are collected. Collecting is normally illegal on state lands, but specimens may be collected legally on private property with the landowner's permission.

The proper identification of fossils by their scientific names can also be rewarding. Books in local libraries or those available from the Florida State Geological Survey will aid in identification. A good reference for beginners is *Florida's Fossils* by Robin C. Brown (Revised Edition 1996, Pineapple Press, Sarasota, Florida).

Venice Archives & Area Historical Collection

happened. The new human creature survived and flourished, but many of the beasts with whom it had coexisted for a thousand or so years died out. Gone were the mastodons, woolly mammoths, saber-toothed tigers, camels, horses, and other wonderful animals of the past. What caused this great extinction? Why did humans survive while other creatures could not live in this new paradise?

The evidence indicates that humans may have been involved in the disappearance of a few of these creatures. Many of the animals were hunted for food. There was no way, however, that humans could have been responsible for all the extinctions that occurred in North America and across the globe.

Perhaps the answer to this riddle will never be found. The fact is that when Lake Okeechobee formed some five thousand years ago, those fascinating creatures had long before become extinct and the basic flora and fauna of the region were established much as they are seen today.

The earliest people came to Florida some twelve thousand years ago, but they did not settle at Lake Okeechobee because there was no lake at that time. The interior of the peninsula was an inhospitable place with little water. Elsewhere, however, where conditions were more favorable, permanent villages were established. Up in the Big Bend area near the Gulf of Mexico coast where peninsular Florida merges with the Panhandle, there is an underwater archaeological site called Page-Ladson. This site indicates the presence of humans well over ten thousand years ago.

The location of Page-Ladson seems logical. Since water in the interior was scarce, the early settlers would have set up their camps nearer sea level where low areas would receive a better supply of fresh water and food would be more abundant. Perhaps, even earlier sites than Page-Ladson will be found someday, lying deep underwater and far out into the Gulf, even closer to the old shoreline that existed when sea level was lower.

More evidence of early human presence in Florida comes from the Little Salt Spring and Warm Mineral Springs in Sarasota County. Skeletal remains from these fascinating springs have been dated at over ten thousand years old. At the time early people lived here, during the last Ice Age when sea level was hundreds of feet lower than it is today, these springs were dry caves that were used for shelter and burials.

Later, the roofs of the caves collapsed, forming sinkholes over two hundred feet deep. Several different species of Ice Age animals fell to their deaths in these sinkholes. Finally, as the earth warmed and sea level rose, the sinks filled with water to become flowing springs. The evolution of Little Salt Spring and Warm Mineral Springs is a story rich in geology, paleontology, and archaeology.

Nomads and hunters undoubtedly traversed the area that was to become Lake Okeechobee. Probably some early people lived here, but no settlement has been discovered by archaeologists that predates a thousand years before Christ was born.

Early humans witnessed the creation of this mighty body of water as slowly increasing rainfall and stream input filled the shallow spoon-shaped depression. This huge puddle of life-giving liquid soon became a mecca for plants and animals. People came to reap its benefits.

Time passed. Birds filled the air. Fishes, turtles, otters, alligators, and other wildlife multiplied. The lake began to teem with life. During the rainy season, its southern bank overflowed and water inched south across a great swamp which also was full of living things.

People came more frequently to the lake to hunt and fish. Eventually, they learned how to kill the scaly-backed alligators by driving a long, sharpened pole down their throats. Soon they would live on its shores and give the mighty lake a name, but it would not be Okeechobee.

2 First Settlers

Settlements began to sprout around Lake Okeechobee at least three thousand years ago. The earliest villages probably appeared just after the lake started to form, some five thousand years ago. However, there is no supportive archaeological evidence older than the three-thousand year date.

Several mounds from native-inhabited sites are found in the Lake Okeechobee area. These mounds were for burials, "kitchen middens" (refuse of shells, bones, and other debris discarded from meals), or served as elevated living areas. Four of the most noteworthy archaeological sites (mounds) known at this time are Chosen (Belle Glade), Fort Center, Big Mound, and Ortona.

The Chosen/Belle Glade site, located near the town of Belle Glade, was excavated by the Smithsonian Institute in 1933 and yielded a number of interesting artifacts. Archaeologists uncovered pottery, arrowheads, spear points, cups, spoons, a deer headdress, and the remains of house posts, suggesting a raised dwelling. This site indicates that pre-Columbian people lived here.

Excavation at Chosen revealed that the bottom of one of the mounds was directly on bedrock. When the first white settlers came here, twelve feet of muck covered the bedrock. Muck is the organic-rich debris that accumulates at the bottom of wetlands from decaying plant material. When the waters are drained and the muck dries, an ideal black soil for growing sugarcane and vegetables remains. The Chosen find demonstrates that natives lived here before any wetlands covered this particular area. Apparently, as the wetlands encroached, they built their living quarters progressively higher.

The Fort Center site, located a couple of miles upstream from Lake Okeechobee on the bank of Fisheating Creek, is another well-known archaeological site with evidence of early people. An elaborate ceremonial/mortuary platform and many other artifacts found at the Fort Center site are indications of a highly advanced culture as far back as two thousand years ago.

During the Seminole Wars the military established a fort here named Fort Center, or Fort Crieter, as it was once referred to. The choice for the fort was along Fisheating Creek and it was logically built on the highest ground in the area — the mounds of the early natives.

Fort Center was later to become notorious as a base for the "boat companies" which were quasi-military groups that captured Seminole Indians for government bounties. Men, women, and children were rounded up by the nefarious boat companies and shipped west to Indian Territory.

Amateur diggers poked around the Fort Center mounds for years, but it was not until 1961 that any scientific investigation began. Many interesting artifacts were uncovered, including a crude map etched on a shell and presumed made by a Spanish captive.

Shark teeth with holes drilled through them were found in abundance which suggests the teeth were used for jewelry or trade. Perhaps these people were bird worshipers because many bird totems and other avian figures were uncovered.

The early Fort Center inhabitants grew corn, a sign of an agricultural civilization. Considering the advanced state of their society, some archaeologists have assumed that people lived here long before two thousand years ago.

In the upper layers of the Fort Center site, many ornaments and trinkets of silver, gold, and copper were excavated

— some crafted by Incas. There were also a few gold and silver bars. Gold ornaments were discovered at the Chosen site. Although none of these precious metals were mined in Florida, they reached the hands of native Floridians after Spanish treasure ships began to be shipwrecked along the coasts.

At present, the Fort Center site is off limits to the public to prevent further vandalism of the property. The owners of the land, Lykes Brothers, Inc., are interested in making this area a state park with a museum displaying the artifacts unearthed.

A mound has been reported near the present town of Okeechobee, and a complex of over thirty mounds is rumored to lie in the cane fields near Clewiston. There are numerous other mounds farther from the shores of Lake Okeechobee. Big Mound, a large network of elevated sites, is located east of Pahokee, nearer the Atlantic coast. Several mounds have been found along the Caloosahatchee River. In fact, there are literally thousands of ancient mounds in southern Florida. Most of them are located along streams, rivers, and lakes.

Early settlers on the east side of Lake Okeechobee were from a small tribe called the Mayaimis, and they called the mighty body of water Lake Mayaimi. Calusa Indians, a ferocious tribe that inhabited much of southwest Florida, lived on the west side of Lake Okeechobee.

Names of the native tribes in Florida are derived from Spaniards listening to the tribal names and repeating them as closely as they could in phonetic Spanish. Sometimes there was a little confusion in the final spelling. Was it Calusa, Calosa, or Caloosa?

For many generations, the early people lived around the shores of Lake Mayaimi, enjoying the gifts from the bountiful lake. They lived on mounds and in houses set on high poles to be safe from the occasionally rising waters. Until newcomers came to spoil their paradise, life was good.

THE ORTONA MOUNDS

The Ortona Mounds near the town of Ortona, approximately fourteen miles west of Moore Haven on State Route 78, are some of the most interesting early Indian Mounds in the Lake Okeechobee area. These are the only mounds that can be easily visited. Take U.S. Route 27 six miles west of Moore Haven to the Junction of Route 27 with State Route 78. Follow Route 78 west eight and two-tenths miles, and just past the Ortona Cemetery, turn right and proceed two-tenths miles to the Ortona Indian Mound Park. This is a delightful little park with picnic facilities, other amenities, and a visitors center (unmanned) with information about the mound complex. A short boardwalk leads over the mounds to a fishing pier on a small lake. Two prehistoric canoe canals, representing the longest man-made prehistoric waterways in North America, led from here to Lake Flirt (now drained) and the Calooshatchee River. At least as early as three thousand years before the present, the Ortona Mounds were occupied. By AD 1200, a huge temple mound was built that stood twenty-two feet tall, creating the highest elevation in Glades County. For unknown reasons, the Ortona site was abandoned sometime between AD 1500 and 1650.

3 Newcomers Arrive

According to some historians and writers, the first European ship to sail along the coast of Florida recorded observations about the land and the abundant fishes in the waters. It was 1497 and the vessel was from Bristol, England, captained by the Venetian, John Cabot. Other historians are not so sure that Cabot ever sailed in Florida waters. Most, however, agreed that no other notable Europeans came here until 1513 when the ex-governor of Puerto Rico, Juan Ponce de León, arrived. He landed somewhere along the coast, probably on the Atlantic side, although it's unclear just where. It seems that every spring and lake in Florida has at one time or another claimed that Ponce de León came there to seek an elusive Fountain of Youth.

Could it have been Lake Mayaimi, later named Lake Okeechobee, that was the sacred water rumored among the natives? Alas, probably not. The word "fountain" is more suggestive of a spring or stream than a lake. Perhaps the fabled water of eternal youth was Warm Mineral Springs, near Venice, about sixty-five miles west of Lake Okeechobee. Even today, people claim that its soothing waters are a wonderful remedy for a tired, aching body. And, from archaeological digs, we know that ancient man inhabited the area around Warm Mineral Springs for thousands of years.

There are over three hundred springs throughout Florida, but nearly all are cool and hardly remind one of restorative waters. Warm Mineral Springs is one of the few springs where waters are warm, rising from deep within the earth where they have been heated by hot bedrock.

But Juan Ponce de León was not here to look for a Fountain of Youth. According to most historians today, that was a myth later associated with Ponce. He was looking for two other things — gold and slaves. Gold was sought to feed the royal coffers in Madrid and to line Ponce de León's pockets. Slaves were needed to work the mines and fields on the settled islands of the Caribbean. The native Caribs died quickly from the white man's diseases, overwork, and starvation. The Spaniards wanted a new supply of labor.

But long before Ponce de León arrived, the natives of Florida knew about the Spaniards' ways. Communications had existed for hundreds of years between the natives of Florida and those of the Caribbean. They traded with each other and probably sold women, children, and their own slaves as well. When the Ponce de León expedition arrived, it was greeted by at least one Indian who understood Spanish, possibly an escapee from Caribbean slavery.

So Juan Ponce de León was not a welcome visitor when he came that day in 1513. He first saw land shortly after the flowery festival of Pascua Florida, or flowery Easter, so he promptly named the new land "La Florida" and claimed it for Spain. Except for a few scattered wild blooms, Ponce found no flowery things when he landed. He thought La Florida was a large island, perhaps like Cuba.

According to some historians, Ponce de León and his men poked and prodded up and down the Atlantic, as far north as Cape Canaveral. They returned south along the Keys which Ponce named "Las Martires" (the martyrs), because, from offshore, they looked like suffering people. It is said the explorers went through or around the Keys and up into Florida Bay to Cape Romano near the Ten Thousand Islands, mapping the land and rivers as they went.

Nearly everywhere they landed, they were met with hostility and some of Ponce's men were wounded. In turn, the

Spaniards killed a few Indians. Not a good beginning for the discoverers of Florida. Finally, near the end of September 1513, they sailed home to Puerto Rico, empty-handed, without gold or slaves. It would be eight years before Juan Ponce de León came back to Florida.

In 1521, Ponce de León returned and, this time, his intention was to establish a settlement. Prepared to stay, he came ashore somewhere along the Gulf coast with his men and equipment. The Calusa, however, attacked the party with such ferocity that many Spaniards were killed and Ponce himself was wounded. The expedition retreated and sailed to Havana where Juan Ponce de León died a few days later from his wound.

It was 1528 before Spain again sent a significant expedition to Florida. This time the group was led by Captain Pánfilo de Narváez. Landing near the present site of Tampa, Narváez set off on foot with three hundred men, traveling north along the coast as he explored and looked for treasure. None was found, and Narváez and most of his men perished. Only four soldiers survived. This small group, which included Cabeza de Vaca, who later wrote about his ordeal, made their way around the Gulf of Mexico and south into Mexico.

A young man by the name of Juan Ortíz was captured by the Indians when the Narváez party first came to the Tampa area. He remained a captive until rescued by Hernando de Soto in 1539. During his years of captivity, Ortíz traveled around much of south Florida. Perhaps he was the first European to lay eyes on Lake Mayaimi.

If it was not Ortíz who was the first European to see the great inland lake, it was probably another white slave of the Indians. Spaniards were not the only ones who practiced slavery in this area. Indians had their own slaves and many of them were Spaniards who had been shipwrecked along the dangerous coasts.

The first recorded account of Lake Mayaimi comes from a Spaniard who was shipwrecked in 1545 at the age of thirteen and lived among the Indians for seventeen years. This man, Escalante de Fontaneda, wrote about numerous small villages, of up to thirty or forty inhabitants each, scattered around Lake Mayaimi. The people ate large-mouth bass, trout, alligator tails, and eels. Coontie flour, made from the root of a cycad plant, was another staple of the Indians.

To fill in the mysterious space on the maps made in the early days, many Spanish cartographers simply scrawled across southern Florida the name "El Laguno del Espíritu Santo" (the Lagoon of the Holy Spirit).

Life on the lake was probably good in those early days when few people other than local inhabitants knew about its

THE NATIVES BECOME EXTINCT

When Juan Ponce de León first arrived in 1513, there were perhaps as many as one hundred thousand native Americans in Florida (some estimates are as high as two hundred thousand). Well-organized tribes lived from the Panhandle to the Keys. To the north, there were the Apalachees and Timucuans; near Tampa, Tocobagas; along the Gulf Coast farther south, Calusas; and in the Keys, Tequestas. They lived in palm-thatched houses clustered in villages. Mounds were built for elevated living areas and burials. Canals were dug for canoe transportation. By the mid 1800s, all of these proud people had disappeared. Not a single person survives that can claim to be a direct descendant of any of these tribes. European disease and massacres took a heavy toll. Many of the natives were sent south into the Caribbean as slaves, either to die or eventually be integrated into the Caribs, their origins lost forever. The English, who ruled Florida for twenty years from 1763 to 1783, treated the natives no better than did the Spaniards. In 1783, the Spaniards regained control and they eventually ceded Florida to the United States in 1821. By then, the native people were nearly extinct. The few remaining, referred to as "Spanish Indians," would soon lose the last of their identity. In a short time the only Indians living in Florida would be Seminoles, who were late arrivals on the scene.

existence. Apparently, the lake people lived peacefully for the next couple of hundred years. Then they vanished.

As late as 1837, the rumored great "inland sea" of Florida was still virtually unknown except to a handful of Seminoles and whites. According to one authority on Florida at the time, he could find no one who had actually seen this mysterious body of water. And a detailed map of Florida published in 1837 failed to indicate the lake. Then, suddenly, the name "Lake Okeechobee" flashed across the new nation.

The Seminoles, who gave Lake Okeechobee its name, were recent immigrants from Georgia where they had broken away from the Creeks. The name "Seminole" means "renegade." Some were called Muskogees and Mikasuki, after the language they spoke. But when it came to fighting the white man, they were all the same — Seminoles.

The Georgia/Florida border had been an uneasy one for years prior to the United States acquiring Florida in 1821. In fact, the brief First Seminole Indian War began in 1817, when General Andrew Jackson began a campaign into northern Florida against Indians and runaway slaves. Seeking asylum,

THE BATTLE OF OKEECHOBEE

The Battle of Okeechobee was fought on the northeastern shore about a mile east of Taylor Creek. The federal forces, led by Zachary Taylor, suffered twenty-six dead and 112 wounded. The Seminoles, led by Chiefs Coacoochee, Alligator, and Arpeika, had an estimated twelve dead and nine wounded. Despite the lopsided casualties, the large federal force of over a thousand men forced the much smaller Indian group to withdraw and Taylor claimed a victory. As news of the "victory" spread, "Okeechobee" became a new household word in the young nation. Although the Second Seminole Indian War dragged on for several more years, the Battle of Okeechobee was its last major engagement.

The Seminoles did accomplish something else in the Battle of Okeechobee. The vast body of water would now be known forevermore as Lake Okeechobee — "Big Water."

slaves crossed the U.S./Florida boundary to live with the Seminoles. Raids into Florida to capture slaves were common. When the United States obtained Florida, the government quickly initiated a plan to clear all of northern Florida of Indians. The government set aside land in the west for the Indians, and efforts were made to resettle Seminoles there. Many were forced to follow the "Trail of Tears" to Indian Territory in Arkansas and Oklahoma. Others who fought to remain in Florida were pushed south, mostly into the Lake Okeechobee and Everglades areas.

Later, a seven-year period of continuous warfare between the federal government and the Seminoles began. This period of fighting, from 1835 to 1842, was called the Second Seminole Indian War. Using guerrilla tactics, the Seminoles found Lake Okeechobee to be a safe haven for their forces. Few white men had ever penetrated into this inhospitable southern end of Florida. The Seminoles could conduct raids when they pleased and return to this refuge. But in 1837, a young colonel by the name of Zachary Taylor led an expedition into the area in pursuit of some runaway Indians and, on Christmas Day, fought a fierce battle on the shore of Lake Okeechobee.

4   Development of Okeechobeeland

After the Battle of Okeechobee in 1837, it was more than fifty years before significant numbers of European descendants saw the "inland sea" again. Cursory surveys were made, including one in 1856 by the Army's Lieutenant Ives who published the first relatively accurate map of Lake Okeechobee and the nearby area. Hunters, trappers, fishermen, and squatters slowly began to move into the area around the lake, sharing it with the few remaining Seminoles. What those early visitors and settlers found was a much different Lake Okeechobee and surrounding countryside than is seen today.

Along the lakeshore, especially the north side, there were forests of slash pine, live oak, and cypress. The southern shore had its own unique ecosystem. On the southern rim, a dense stand of custard apple trees grew, draped with moon vines. This strange floral growth extended southward for a couple of miles and covered the entire lakeshore, as well as the islands. Several islands are found within the southern waters of Lake Okeechobee. The largest of these were to be named Ritta, Kreamer, Torry, and Observation Islands.

Another characteristic of the southern shore was the many "deadend rivers" that led south from Lake Okeechobee. These were distributaries, i.e., they distributed excess water out of the lake. When the lake water was high in the rainy season, these rivers channeled the overflow south into the Everglades. At least seventeen deadend rivers were counted by an early surveyor. Some were wide and navigable where they exited the lake, but they extended only short distances before disappearing as their waters spread across the broad swampland.

South of the custard apple forests on the southern shore and circling most of the rest of Lake Okeechobee, except along part of the north side, lay extensive saw grass prairies of swampland with their bottoms composed of rich organic muck accumulated over the eons. These swamps resembled much of today's saw grass Everglades where the marvelous biomass *periphyton*, a brownish-green scum, serves as the base of the food chain.

The lake and adjacent area teemed with wildlife. Bears, panthers, bobcats, raccoons, deer, and possums foraged along the shores while alligators, otters, muskrats, and fish filled the waters. According to early visitors to this area, flocks of birds were so thick that they darkened the skies. All this — the muck lands, the flora, and the fauna — were natural resources waiting to be exploited.

Only a handful of whites and Seminoles lived in the Lake Okeechobee area late in the nineteenth century, and no serious development had yet begun. Okeechobeeland was then truly one of the last frontiers left in the United States. But by 1882, things began to change rapidly.

In that year, the first dredges began their work. Wetlands were considered undesirable in those days and were drained where possible to turn them into profitable agricultural and grazing lands.

The first serious dredging in southern Florida was along the Kissimmee River, the major stream flowing into Lake Okeechobee, to make it navigable for steamboats. Since there was no outlet from the lake, it was connected by dredging to the Caloosahatchee River. This provided navigation all the way from Lake Kissimmee (near Orlando), down the Kissimmee River, across Lake Okeechobee, down the Caloosahatchee River, and into the Gulf of Mexico at Fort Myers.

WEST SIDE The "canalized" Caloosahatchee River
Photo courtesy of South Florida Water Management District

A period of economic depression in 1893 dried up funds temporarily, but dredging soon continued in earnest. The Miami Canal, extending eighty miles from the southern shore of Lake Okeechobee to the east coast at Miami, was begun in the late 1890s but not completed until the early 1900s. In 1921, the forty-mile St. Lucie Canal to the east coast was dug. The St. Lucie Canal completed the Cross Florida Waterway (Okeechobee Waterway) allowing boats to travel from the Atlantic Ocean, across Lake Okeechobee, and down the Caloosahatchee River into the Gulf of Mexico.

More hunters and trappers began to arrive, and the animal population of the lake area was rapidly depleted. Egrets were slain by the thousands for their valuable aigrettes, the plumes that adorned the hats of fashionable ladies of those days. Ducks, geese, limpkins, and other birds were hunted for food. Otters, raccoons, bears, panthers, and bobcats were trapped for their fur, and alligators were sought for their hides.

No doubt there were some enormous alligators taken from the lake in those days. Early explorers in Florida had described alligators that were longer than twenty feet.

Reportedly, the largest known alligator in recent times was just over nineteen feet. In fact, the largest taken out of Lake Okeechobee was said to be about nineteen feet long. Some modern scientific researchers, however, dispute these claims. They believe that alligators seldom, if ever, have exceeded about thirteen feet. Even so, thirteen feet is an awesome size for an alligator.

While the exact size of the largest alligators may be questionable, there surely were large ones in the past. Alligators grow throughout their lifetimes, and the big ones were the ones most sought by early hunters. Because hunting decreased their numbers sharply in the first half of this century, probably few alligators today are more than forty years old, but many were presumably older than that when settlers first came to Okeechobee. The life span of an alligator is believed by some naturalists to exceed fifty years.

The big cash crop from the lake, however, became catfish. With navigation available to the Gulf, steamboats began ferrying loads of catfish to Fort Myers. When the railroad came to Okeechobee City in 1915, catfish were hauled out by the boxcar.

Lumbering was a short-lived business on the north shore as land was cleared. The huge stands of cypress, oak, and pine were decimated, allowing beef and dairy cattle to graze. Okeechobee County became the biggest dairy area in the state.

On the south shore, the custard apple trees and moon vines were cut to create farmland. As the swamps were

"SELLING LAND BY THE GALLON"

Even before the land was drained, promoters sold small tracts of wetlands on the promise that it would be drained to expose "soil richer than the Nile Valley." Many investors lost their money on these land schemes, and soon the word "Everglades" became nearly synonymous with "swindle."

drained to expose the muck, farms began to sprout around the lake, and crops were grown on the islands. Small towns developed. Moore Haven, Clewiston, Belle Glade, and Pahokee became important communities in the southern sector of the lake area while Okeechobee City was the hub of activity on the north shore.

For the farms that survived, sugarcane became an important cash crop. The black soil of the muck lands and the warm climate made ideal growing conditions for cane. Winter vegetables were also important. Minor industries, such as the production of turpentine from pine trees, were established. Spanish moss was gathered and sold for mattress and furniture stuffing.

The fortunes of the Lake Okeechobee people rose and fell through the early years. Floods, frosts, and lack of the drainage which had been promised by promoters and the state ruined many of them. Many farmers and other settlers were wiped out by devastating hurricanes.

Moore Haven, a thriving farmer's town on the southwest shore, was only eleven years old in 1926. Because the town was prone to flooding when the lake level became too high, an earthen levee had been constructed along the periphery of the lake in that area. This protective dike became a death trap for Moore Haven.

In September 1926, a hurricane which had only hours earlier laid waste to the city of Miami, roared into the Lake Okeechobee area. As the storm approached, a surveyor working on the east side of the lake some thirty miles from Moore Haven noticed something unusual. Although the water was normally ten feet deep where he was working, the surveyor could now see an exposed lake bottom reaching out a considerable distance from the normal shoreline. The exposed bottom was caused by the lake water being tilted westward by the force of the wind. Consequently, water was piling up against the Moore Haven levee. Finally, the makeshift dike burst. The resulting flood that swept through town killed over 150 people (some estimates have been as high as 250). Two years later, in the same month as the 1926 hurricane, the Lake Okeechobee area was hit again, this time much harder.

In September 1928, as the area was still recovering from the 1926 storm, Lake Okeechobee was hit by another powerful hurricane. This time, over twenty-five hundred lost their lives, almost all within an hour's time. This gave Lake Okeechobee the dubious distinction of being the site of the third worst tragedy ever to occur within the United States — topped only by the Galveston, Texas, hurricane and the Johnstown, Pennsylvania, flood losses.

After the terrible loss of life in 1928, most residents of the Lake Okeechobee area agreed that something had to be done quickly to prevent the recurrence of hurricane disasters. Some people favored the elimination of all dikes around the lake and the reconstruction of the towns on higher ground. From the standpoint of long-term environmental effects, perhaps, that would have been the best solution. However, the majority was in favor of building a bigger and better levee.

NORTH SIDE   The Henry Creek Lock on the northern shore of Lake Okeechobee. The great Herbert Hoover Dike separates the rim canal on the right from Lake Okeechobee on the left.   Photo courtesy of South Florida Water Management District

Prior to his inauguration in 1929, President-elect Herbert Hoover visited the site of destruction. Hoover, a geological engineer, was in favor of a new dike. As a result of his support, the U.S. Army Corps of Engineers began a massive levee building effort in 1930. The project was essentially completed in 1937 and, in the ensuing years, there have been considerable improvements made along the dike. Today, this great earthen work stands at an average elevation of thirty-four feet and extends one hundred and ten miles around Lake Okeechobee. Along the western and northwestern shores of the lake, secondary dikes connected to the Hoover Dike extend away from the lake and for some distance up the sides of the Kissimmee River, the Fisheating Creek floodplain, the Indian Prairie Canal, and the Harney Pond Canal. Except for these four major inputs, the Herbert Hoover Dike completely encloses Lake Okeechobee.

Several hurricanes have since passed over the Lake Okeechobee area and no significant damage has occurred. The grateful citizens of the lake dedicated the massive levee at Clewiston on January 12, 1961. Herbert Hoover attended the ceremony, and the levee was designated the "Herbert Hoover Dike" in appreciation of the man whose vision and support made it possible.

Although the levee has held firm against hurricanes and flooding, there is no guarantee that it can permanently resist Mother Nature. In 1995, heavy rainfall raised the level of the lake to near record heights of over eighteen and a half feet. The highest recorded level is 18.77 feet in 1947. Fortunately, although the heavy rains of 1995 occurred at the end of the hurricane season, no serious storm accompanied the high water. It is possible that some time in the future a combination of high lake water and hurricane force winds could cause extensive damage. Presently, however, most residents around the lake feel fairly secure behind the dike.

Another huge engineering feat was accomplished in the Lake Okeechobee area. The Kissimmee River, the largest input

NORTH SIDE   "Canalized" Kissimmee River. Old river channel
with its meanders is to the right.   Photo courtesy of South
Florida Water Management District

stream into Lake Okeechobee, was a twisting, meandering
waterway with a wide marshy floodplain. The river and the
adjoining lands teemed with wildlife. Travelers on the river
were enthusiastic about the beautiful bird life and other wild
animals they observed.

In September 1947, the area was hit by another big hurricane — this one causing extensive flooding along the Kissimmee River valley. Hundreds of cattle drowned, and residents again asked for federal help. Funds were authorized by Congress in 1948, and the U.S. Army Corps of Engineers began work in 1950. With high flood-control dikes that extend for miles along both sides of the river, the Kissimmee was essentially converted to a canal ("Canal 38") over fifty miles long, thirty feet deep, and more than three hundred feet wide.

Almost from the beginning, the "canalization" of the Kissimmee River generated controversy. Not only had the floodplain marshes provided a wonderful wildlife sanctuary, the meanders of the river had served as a natural filtration system, which kept harmful pollutants out of Lake Okeechobee and the Everglades. Without nature's filtering, the ecosystems of both these natural wonders became endangered.

The environmental damage caused by straightening the Kissimmee River was soon apparent and, by the early 1970s, there was a strong movement underway to restore the original meanders. This reclamation is underway today. The largest such project ever attempted in the world, it will be an enormous "un-engineering" task that will cost hundreds of millions of dollars and take years to complete. In fact, the job is so complex that one legislator likened the project to "attempting to unscramble an egg." This endeavor, like most large scale projects, has both supporters and opponents. However, the fact is growing in the consciousness of Florida and the nation that something needs to be done soon to save the Everglades.

5 Notable Names from the Past

*T*he Lake Okeechobee area has had its share of colorful characters in the past — some good people, some not so good. Here are a few of them:

"Old Rough and Ready"

Perhaps the closest that Florida has come to having a native son as a president of the United States was Zachary Taylor. Although he was born in Virginia, the path that took Taylor to the highest office in the land began at Lake Okeechobee: he commanded the Federal forces at the famous Battle of Okeechobee during the Second Seminole Indian War.

Coacoochee, "The Wildcat," the son of a chief, was tricked into capture under a false flag of truce offered by federal troops in 1837 and sent to prison at St. Augustine. There, it is said, he and several of his men slowly starved themselves until they were thin enough to slip out of their cells. Gathering more followers as they went, the Seminoles headed south toward Lake Okeechobee.

Colonel Zachary Taylor, head of the garrison at Tampa, was ordered to pursue Coacoochee. After Taylor marched his troops to Lake Kissimmee, he established Fort Garner. Then, he continued south along the Kissimmee River to a point about twenty miles from the lake where he left artillery and other equipment at a hastily-constructed stockade he named Fort Bassinger. He learned that the Seminoles were camped near Lake Okeechobee, so Taylor set off with over a thousand men toward the lake.

Three to four hundred Seminoles, led by Cocacoochee and other chiefs, were waiting for Taylor. Concealed in a cypress hammock surrounded by a saw grass prairie through which they had cut an access path to their hiding place, the Seminoles hoped to lure the troops down that path to an ambush. The troops obliged and the battle was fought on Christmas Day, 1837.

Although the Federal losses were greater than those of the Seminoles, the overwhelming number of troops finally forced the Indians to withdraw, and Taylor claimed victory. The news spread quickly, and people finally became aware of the existence of Lake Okeechobee.

The battle took place near a large creek on the northern shore. Colonel Taylor later had this stream, which is one of the three principal natural inlets into the lake, named after him. He was also given his nickname "Old Rough and Ready" as a result of the encounter. According to one of his men, Taylor was called this "because he treated the redskins in the roughest way and in the readiest manner." Further, he was promoted to Brigadier General.

Although Zachary Taylor was to distinguish himself even more in the Mexican War, his fame originated at Lake Okeechobee. Taylor went on to become the twelfth president of the United States.

Coacoochee was once again captured under a treacherous flag of truce and exiled west to Indian Territory.

"Ham" Disston

Hamilton Disston loved to fish and made his first trip to Florida in 1877. A few years later, this bold young man was the sole owner of four million acres of Florida land, including all of Lake Okeechobee. Consequently, at the age of thirty-seven, Ham Disston became the largest landowner in the United States.

Born on August 23, 1844, Hamilton Disston was the son of the successful owner and founder of Keystone Saw, Tool, Steel and File Works in Philadelphia. Upon the event of his father's death Ham inherited the company. He was thirty-four years old. Like his father, Ham was a good businessman, and the company prospered under his leadership.

The state of Florida was still reeling from the Civil War and deeply in debt near the turn of the century. One way to raise money was to sell public lands, and the state found a buyer in young Disston. On May 30, 1881, Disston bought four million acres for twenty-five cents an acre. Proclaiming that "No other transaction has been of greater service to the state," the governor was jubilant. The *Tallahassee Weekly* lamented, "Would that the state of Florida had a thousand Disstons!"

However, there were critics. Some said that Florida made a bad deal. The state was supposed to have sold only swampland to Disston but, actually, much of the land was high and dry. And what would happen to the poor squatters already on the land? Fortunately, Disston allowed most of the settlers to buy their homes and land for reasonable prices. He set out to do his own building on this new land and to reclaim swamplands. First, however, Disston sold half his holdings for six hundred thousand dollars to obtain working capital.

His remaining two million acres extended from near Orlando south across Lake Okeechobee and twenty-five miles farther into the Everglades. It included a strip on each side of the Caloosahatchee River all the way to the Gulf of Mexico.

The earliest monumental engineering feats in southern Florida were the dredging of existing waterways and the digging of canals. This work drained the swamps and lakes, provided transportation routes, and allowed a water supply to reach urban areas. The canals seem to be everywhere and literally thousands of miles of them exist today in southern Florida. Many of these canals are now considered to have been ill-advised and harmful to the environment.

Hamilton Disston began dredging on his land in 1882 and, by August 1884, the state engineer reported that over two million acres of Disston's land and adjoining acreage had been permanently drained. Canals and/or deepwater channels were dug between several lakes and from Lake Kissimmee into the Kissimmee River. In the southwestern part of Lake Okeechobee, starting at the present site of Moore Haven, a canal between the Caloosahatchee River and the lake was opened. Thus was created a passageway from the Gulf of Mexico coast near Fort Myers, up the Caloosahatchee, into Lake Okeechobee, up the Kissimmee River, and into Lake Kissimmee. Further, half the Cross Florida Waterway (later named the Okeechobee Waterway) was now complete.

With all this new drainage, the level of various lakes was lowered, leaving thousand of acres of dry muck lands where once there were wet saw grass prairies. Disston began planting sugarcane on these old lake and swamp beds and formed the St. Cloud Sugar Plantation Company with a big sugar mill at St. Cloud.

Ham sold more land, brought in new settlers, and assisted them in getting started with their farms. Along with them he experimented in the raising of livestock, vegetables, fruit, rice, and even tobacco.

In the meantime, dredging continued. Disston had several ambitious plans. One was to lower the water level on Lake Okeechobee and drain the Everglades. Another was to create a navigable trans-Florida waterway from Jacksonville, down the St. Johns River, into Lake Kissimmee, down the Kissimmee River, across Lake Okeechobee, and down the Caloosahatchee River to the Gulf. Along this waterway he hoped to create "one of the most popular tourist routes in the world." One supporter said, "The day may come when you will see ocean steamers pass over the Okeechobee route from the Gulf to the Atlantic." Another of Ham's plans was to dig a canal from the south end of Lake Okeechobee ninety miles south to Shark River in the Everglades. Still another was to build a railroad from Kissimmee to the Gulf.

Disston died unexpectedly in 1896, at the age of fifty-two. His heirs refused to continue working on the Florida project, and land that did not revert to the state for uncollected taxes was eventually sold for only seventy thousand dollars.

Had Hamilton Disston lived a longer life and had the economy improved, there's little doubt that this ambitious visionary would have drained all of south Florida. Of course, there would have been no Everglades and, perhaps, not even a Lake Okeechobee.

Pogey Bill

William E. Collins, also known as Pogey Bill, arrived on the Lake Okeechobee scene in 1910 from Tampa and went to work as a fisherman. He quickly became known as the toughest catfisherman who ever busted up the town of Tantie (the early name for Okeechobee) on a drunken Saturday night. In those days, when the fishermen, cowboys, hunters, and timbermen met in town, there was always a good fight or two to liven up things. In one of these altercations, Pogey Bill had a finger bitten off.

Pogey Bill was a natural leader with a magnetic personality and a heart of gold. He made good money from catfishing and gambling, but it seems he always gave his money to some needy soul. The name "Pogey" came from his attempt once to sell some pogey fish that were unfit for consumption. Tired of his drunken rampages, town officials were finally able to arrest Pogey Bill and sentence him to ninety days in jail at Fort Pierce. There was such a public outcry over his arrest that the judge reconsidered. The judge and Dr. Anner, the "Squaw Doc," went to visit Pogey Bill in his cell. After talking to Pogey at length, they were able to obtain his promise to reform as a condition for his release.

Becoming a model citizen, Pogey Bill was soon given the job of marshal of Okeechobee and shortly thereafter was elected sheriff of Okeechobee County, a position he held for fourteen years. He married but had no children and spent a great deal of his time and money helping the youngsters of Okeechobeeland.

Pogey Bill organized a baseball team and a Boy Scout troop, and bought gloves to teach boys boxing. He continued to help folks in need and strictly enforced the law except, perhaps, in the making of moonshine. Bootleggers were not permitted to run wild, but Pogey Bill seemed to look the other way much of the time. He was not a believer in Prohibition, but it was said that he kept Scarface Al Capone's gang out of town. Apparently, they wanted to expand their illegal liquor operations to include Okeechobee County. Pogey Bill made it clear that they were not welcome.

Shortly after his run-in with the gang Pogey Bill was indicted for guarding a road while moonshine was loaded onto trucks. This spurred rumors that Capone's mob had taken revenge by directing Federal agents to Bill.

After his arrest, he was tried twice in Miami. The first trial ended in a hung jury. He was convicted at the second trial and sentenced to six years in prison. On appeal, he was given six years' probation instead of the jail sentence. Left with no money, Pogey Bill was not able to run a successful campaign for reelection and lost his sheriff's position by three votes.

Pogey Bill later became chief of police in Frostproof, Florida, where he died of pneumonia in 1934. So ended the era of one of Lake Okeechobee's most colorful characters.

"Squaw Doc"

In 1911, a pretty, blond-haired, blue-eyed young woman arrived in what is now Okeechobee with her husband and two children. They came from Chicago, where her husband, Dr. Charles Roy Darrow, had been on the staff of Cook County Hospital. Anna A. Darrow, also a doctor, had passed her medical exam with the highest grades ever made up to that time. She became the second female physician licensed in Florida.

The family came primarily to find a warmer climate for the husband, who had developed a heart condition. Roy, as his friends called him, stayed in town to practice medicine and operate a drug store. He was "Doc" to his patients but soon he was known as "Mr. Doc Anner."

"Doc Anner," or the "Squaw Doctor," as Anna Darrow was called, made house calls all over the rugged terrain. In a Model T, motorboat, canoe, oxcart, or on foot, Doc Anner went to call on the sick in fish camps, cow camps, lumber camps, and Seminole villages. Usually traveling alone, she went unarmed and unafraid in this wild land. She delivered babies and, occasionally, helped cows give birth. A caring person, she attended weddings of patients, helped them lay out the dead for funerals, and sang at the services.

Often traveling over the thirty miles of rough road to the Seminole camps around Indiantown, she treated the sick but never charged a fee. They always paid her, however, in venison, wild turkeys, or berries, or in some other fashion.

At one time during the early, rapid growth of Okeechobee, about 1914 to 1916, promoters tried to sell the idea of making this new city the capital of Florida, to replace Tallahassee. So seriously was this matter considered by the lake citizens that Doc Anner offered to give the state a tract of land for the capital site.

The Darrows moved to Stuart in 1922 and, while there, Doc Anner was sometimes called on to treat a member of the notorious Ashley-Mobley outlaw gang. In 1924, the Darrows moved to Fort Lauderdale, where Doc Roy died in 1926.

Doc Anner eventually retired to Coral Gables to pursue her longtime hobby of oil painting. She did many scenes of Taylor Creek, the saw grass prairies around Lake Okeechobee, and the Seminoles. Two of her oils were exhibited at the Chicago World's Fair. Her best-known work depicts her leaving the Model T, black bag in hand, and approaching a couple waiting on the porch of a shack. In the painting, she is confronted by a rattlesnake and a mother hen is shown rushing at the snake, squawking and flapping her wings. Overhead, a Florida stork is delivering twin babies, the task Doc Anner had arrived to do in this remote area.

It is fitting that this courageous woman spent the autumn of her life pursuing her favorite hobby. She certainly had earned a comfortable and happy retirement.

"Fingey" Connors

The man who brought the "Tin Lizzie" (the Model T Ford) to Lake Okeechobee, William J. Connors, was a wealthy man from Buffalo, New York. He had risen from the ranks of the stevedores, fighting his way up and suffering a broken finger, which earned him the nickname "Fingey." He was also referred to as "Jiggs," after the famous comic strip of the time. The story goes that George McManus, creator of "Jiggs and Maggie," had wanted to marry Connors' daughter but was rejected by Connors' wife, Maggie. From then on, the comic strip was, reportedly, a characterization of Connors and his wife. They fit the parts perfectly. Fingey was a corned-beef-eating Jiggs type and Maggie was the shrew portrayed in the comic strip.

Connors bought much of the town site of Okeechobee in 1917 and another sixteen thousand acres in the area. His most notable achievement was the construction of a road.

Other Okeechobeelanders

Many other people made significant contributions to the rich history and development of the Lake Okeechobee area. Some, however, like the notorious Jacob E. Mickler, head of one of the boat companies, are not so fondly remembered. The boat companies consisted of volunteer bounty hunters who captured Seminoles and deported them to Indian territory. Mickler operated out of Fort Center on Fisheating Creek.

Marian O'Brien, the "Duchess of Moore Haven," deserves mention. She was elected mayor of Moore Haven in 1918, reportedly the first woman mayor in the United States, and also became president of the bank in Moore Haven.

Billy Bowlegs III was one of the best-known residents of the Brighton Seminole Indian Reservation, located near the northwest shore of Lake Okeechobee. He was not, however, related to the famous Billy Bowlegs who battled the troopers during the Seminole Wars and was later deported to Indian Territory (Oklahoma).

The list of notables could go on and on. For those interested in more details about the people who played important roles in the development of Okeechobeeland, the historical societies around the lake are a great source.

The real pioneers and heroes — those who contributed the most — were the ordinary folks, the "Crackers."

THE CONNORS HIGHWAY

To develop and promote his lands, Connors built a highway from West Palm Beach to Canal Point on the eastern shore of Lake Okeechobee and, from there, some thirty-three miles along the east side of the lake to the town of Okeechobee. Built largely on muck, the road was declared one of the fourteen outstanding engineering achievements in North America for the year 1924 by the Engineering News-Record. Connecting at Okeechobee with pre-existing roads to the Gulf coast, the new Connors Highway provided the first road link from the east to the west coast of Florida. It was a toll road with a charge of $1.50 a car to travel its length. The official opening of the new road was a ribbon-cutting ceremony at Okeechobee on July 4, 1924. A motorcade of some two thousand cars made the trip and fifteen thousand people turned out for the event. Connors was hailed as "The Great Developer" by Governor Gary Hardee. Fingey, who always claimed that he made most of his money by "doing damned fool things," said that his new road was just "another damn fool thing."

Crackers

Many newcomers to Florida are surprised to hear the word Cracker applied to Floridians, thinking that it refers only to people from Georgia. Actually, many of the early settlers were migrants from Georgia seeking new grazing land for their cattle and looking for other opportunities. The origin of the word seems unclear. According to Webster's dictionary, it is a contemptuous term meaning "poor whites." Others attribute it to the cracking of the bullwhips the early cattle drovers used.

Whatever the source of the word, we should admire those hardy souls who braved the elements in this new land and eked a living from it. Many were barefoot, poorly dressed, and uneducated, but they were generally a proud people, ferociously independent, living without government aid, and resourceful enough to better their lives as best they could. One such Cracker, Napoleon Bonaparte Broward, from humble beginnings in northern Florida, went on to become governor of Florida, running on his promise to "Drain the Everglades!"

Part 2 THE PRESENT

6 *Okeechobeeland Today*

*T*oday, despite people's tinkering, Lake Okeechobee remains one of Florida's greatest natural wonders. Its bird life has made a remarkable comeback after being devastated during the plume hunting days and the Great Depression, when, of necessity, so many wildfowl went into the stew pot. Alligators, nearly hunted to extinction, are now thriving. In the Kissimmee River, Fisheating Creek, and other waterways around the lake, river otters are again abundant.

The water of Lake Okeechobee, a brownish color due to tannic acid from prolific organic matter in the watershed, teems with fishes. Sharks, tarpon, dolphin, and snook, normally found in saline waters, sometimes make their way into Lake Okeechobee through the locks on the Caloosahatchee River and the St. Lucie Canal. These alien creatures pass through the locks along with boats. Even manatees, another creature presumably not native to Lake Okeechobee (how could they have gotten into Lake Okeechobee when there were no natural connections to the sea coasts until waterways were dredged?), are occasionally sighted in the lake and streams. Unfortunately, a few of these gentle giants are crushed in the locks each year. It is hoped that newly installed sensors on the lock gates will prevent these tragedies. Although on a limited and controlled scale, there is still a commercial catfishing industry. Bass fishing is a popular sport attracting people from around the world.

EATING LAKE OKEECHOBEE'S FISH

All species of fish taken from Lake Okeechobee are safe for unrestricted consumption, according to the Florida Game and Fresh Water Fish Commission. Many of southern Florida's other lakes, rivers, and coastal bays are so badly polluted that restrictions are placed on the consumption of fish from their waters. Serious pollution (primarily non-toxic phosphates) is present in the big lake but, so far, the fish are safe to eat. The most widely sought fish in Lake Okeechobee for the dinner table is the delicious speckled perch, with the catfish coming in second. While a few small bass are saved for eating and an occasional big one is kept for a trophy, most bass are released after they are caught.

Millions of speckled perch are pulled from the lake each year.

Cattle and dairy farms predominate on the north side of Lake Okeechobee. There has been a large decline recently in the number of dairy farms. Their numbers were reduced because Lake Okeechobee was becoming saturated with nutrient pollutants and dairy farms were considered one of the biggest culprits. The enriched water was finding its way into the Everglades, threatening that fragile ecosystem.

WEST SIDE   Beef cattle in the marshes
Photo courtesy of South Florida Water Management District

According to officials of Everglades National Park, one cow produces as much raw waste daily as do twenty city residents. Dairy cows are considered especially bad because these cows are kept in small restricted areas where they are fed supplemental grains and they produce a manure particularly rich in damaging nutrients. Beef cattle, on the other hand, range over a wider area and are not usually fed much supplemental food.

To reduce the pollution from animal wastes, the state has been buying out dairy farms in the lake's drainage basin. Between 1992 and 1995, the number of dairy farms in Okeechobee County was reduced by one-third. Only twenty-five farms are left. While this doesn't sound like much of a dairy industry, the size of some of the individual farms is staggering.

Now, the few remaining dairy farms in Okeechobee tightly control their nutrient runoff and cause far less environmental damage than in the past.

Runoff from the dairy farms, though not toxic to humans, is fatal to some living organisms in Lake Okeechobee and the

NORTH SIDE: Larsen Dairy Farm, an enormous operation in Okeechobee County

Everglades. As nutrients in the water increase, one of the first transformations is the destruction of periphyton, a marvelous, scummy biomass at the bottom of the food chain. This biomass is perhaps the most important life form in the Everglades because without it, nothing else up the food chain could exist. Subsequently, the saw grass is replaced by cattails, which thrive on elevated nutrient levels. Where once there were great expanses of saw grass in and around Lake Okeechobee, there are now only small, scattered patches.

On the east, south, and southwest sides of the lake, sugar is king. The cane fields are in the old swampland that surrounded much of Lake Okeechobee. Black muck soil, left by the slow accumulation of organic debris in the bottom of swamps, is ideal for cane.

The sugar industry in recent years has fallen under attack for its role in damaging the Everglades. Runoff from the cane fields is thought to be a major cause of pollution in the Everglades. Backpumping from the cane fields into Lake Okeechobee during flood times also contributes to excess nutrient pollution in the lake. Recent reports, however, suggest that nutrient pollution of the Everglades from the cane fields is already being reduced. According to the South Florida Water Management District a human-made 3,500-acre marshland southeast of Lake Okeechobee, built to filter out contaminants, is working better than expected. Additional artificial marshland filters are planned.

The Everglades Forever Act, legislation passed by the state of Florida in 1995, is designed to ease the mounting pollution problems connected with Lake Okeechobee and the Everglades. And the Kissimmee River is the site of the biggest restoration program ever attempted. Beginning in the 1950s, the river was dredged, straightened, canalized, and leveed, and the adjoining floodplains were drained for agriculture. Now, the river is being restored to its original meanders along much of its course. The purpose is to allow the curves to once again function as the natural filters they were originally. It is hoped that the restoration will clean up much of the Kissimmee River water before it reaches Lake Okeechobee.

Slowly but surely, things are changing around Lake Okeechobee. Many folks think the changes are for the better but there are opponents who feel that some of the changes are hurting the economy. The farms and cane fields have been a source of income and employment since development came to Okeechobeeland. These jobs are hard to replace. Some think a new era of ecotourism will provide a needed boost to the area's economy. It is certainly a region of great potential for drawing tourists who are interested in the natural world or love to fish.

Lake Okeechobee is indeed different today than it was when people first arrived here. Fortunately, it remains a truly great natural wonder of Florida. For those who don't fish, there are opportunities to pursue birdwatching, botanical studies, fossil collecting, general nature observation, or to just explore the many attractions around the lake area.

7 Flora

First-time visitors to southern Florida and the Lake Okeechobee area can be somewhat overwhelmed by the lushness of the vegetation. An ocean of greenery confronts them and, superficially, there doesn't seem to be much variety. They can see that the palms are different than northern tree species, but most of the others appear similar. However, on closer examination, the mass of greenery becomes individualized and the abundance of separate species is apparent. In fact, Florida has more tree species than any other state in the continental United States. Of the six hundred or so trees native to North America, nearly three hundred are found in Florida, and this does not include the multitude of introduced exotics.

Although delving deeply into the subject is beyond the scope of this guidebook, some familiarization with the common flora can provide much enjoyment for visitors.

The original flora has been greatly decimated around the lake. The custard apple and moon vine stands of the southern shore were cut to create fields for sugarcane and vegetable crops, while the big stands of cypress, oak, and pine in the north were felled for timber and to clear land for farms. Florida still has a large timber industry that employs some fifty thousand people. More than half the state is covered in forests. Today, most of the cutting is in northern Florida for pulpwood. Not enough timber is left around Lake Okeechobee to make logging worthwhile. However, many lovely native trees remain in the area. Following are a few of them:

Oak (*Quercus*): The generic scientific name for oak, *Quercus*, means "beautiful tree." There are a couple dozen species of oak in Florida. The live oak, *Q. virginiana*, is found statewide, from the tip of the Keys to the northern border.

The live oak is a majestic tree that can reach upwards of ninety feet and grow to more than nine feet in diameter at the base, with its mighty branches beginning a short distance off the ground. This is the stereotypic huge tree draped with Spanish moss that is sometimes seen in Hollywood's version of a southern plantation. It stays green all year, hence the name live oak. However, don't try to tell anyone who has a patio shaded by one of these oaks that they don't shed their leaves. They definitely do! At certain times of the year, particularly after a freeze, these trees seem to rain leaves, especially on windy days. But the live oak may change its leaves so subtly and gradually that there is not an apparent loss of greenery.

A good place to view live oaks is Flagler Park in the center of Okeechobee. These trees were planted by women of the town in the early 1920s. At that time, the young trees had to be protected from grazing cows.

Laurel oak (*Q. hemisphaerica*): This is another stately tree that resembles the live oak (but has a smoother bark) and is also found in the Okeechobee area.

Cabbage palmetto or sabal palm (*Sabal palmetto*): The sabal palm, sometimes misspelled sabel or sable, is Florida's state tree. It is the most common palm around Lake Okeechobee, especially on the northern and western sides. Other names are cabbage palm or swamp cabbage palm, so named because the heart of the tree can be eaten. The Florida black bear has been observed tearing down a sizable sabal palm to get this delicacy. Unfortunately, collecting the heart of a sabal palm kills the tree.

The sabal palm is one of the hardiest of palms and is drought-, freeze-, and saltwater-tolerant. Found throughout the state, it is most readily recognized by its distinctive fan-shaped fronds. For simple identification, palms may be broken into two groups, fan and feather, based on the appearance of their fronds. The fan is a relatively short frond with a spread out fan shape; the feather is a long frond. The sabal palm is a fan palm whereas the royal palm (see below) is a feather palm.

Royal palm (*Roystonea elata*): The royal palm (spelled royal-palm by many naturalists) is the most stately of the Florida palms. This lovely tree grows upward of ninety feet and is easily identified by the shiny, smooth, dark green crown-shaft at the top of the tree trunk. Royal palms line many of Pahokee's streets.

There was a big debate in the 1940s when the legislature was trying to select an official state tree. The House of Representatives initially picked the royal palm, but after further consideration, chose the cabbage palm. The cabbage palm was deemed more appropriate because it has state wide distribution while the royal palm is limited to southern Florida.

Paurotis palm (*Acoelorrhaphe wrightii*): The paurotis palm, also known as the Everglades palm, is a fan palm which grows in distinctive clumps. On the southern shore of Lake Okeechobee, John Stretch Park has many fine examples of paurotis palms.

Pine (*Pinus*): Several species of pine are found across Florida. The most widespread, and the one most common in the Lake Okeechobee area, is the slash pine, *P. elliotti.*

Cypress (*Taxodium*): Scattered remnants of beautiful and once abundant cypress forests can be seen around Lake Okeechobee. Bald cypress (*T. distichum*), so-called for the annual shedding of its needle-like foliage which forms on lateral branchlets, grows one hundred feet to one hundred-twenty feet tall and over ten feet in diameter. Typically a swampland tree, it is not confined to that environment. When growing in water its knobby "knees" protrude above the surface around the base of the tree. The knees are believed

EAST SIDE Cypress trees and their knees in the Barley Barber
Swamp near Indiantown
Photo courtesy of South Florida Water Management District

by some naturalists to serve as aerators for the root system and
are usually not found where the bald cypress grows on high
ground. Scientists, however, are not in complete agreement
about the function of cypress knees. Pond cypress (*T.
distichum* var. *nutans*) is commonly found growing at the
water's edge. Its shorter, flat foliage grows on the slender twigs
of horizontal branches.

Hackberry (Georgia hackberry, *Celtis tenuifolia*): The hackberry, with its small, round, orange-red fruits, grows thirty to forty feet tall and is a favorite roosting site for many Lake Okeechobee birds. Interestingly, native birds do not appear to perch, roost, or nest much in the exotic trees of southern Florida. Perhaps something in the birds' genes tell them to stick with the native trees. Some scientists believe it is a simple matter of the exotic not being as comfortable for the birds. A good example of the lure of the hackberry for roosting can be seen at the west side of Taylor Creek Lock near Okeechobee. Here a small stand of hackberry trees is usually full of turkey vultures, black vultures, and several species of water birds. Nearby, exotic trees like the casuarina are virtually ignored by the birds.

Saw palmetto (*Serenoa repens*): This low-lying fan palm is widespread under pine trees and other forest growths. It resembles somewhat the brakes, or bracken (fern) understory seen in pine forests of the north woods. Older individual palmettos may rise to ten feet or higher on slender trunks (called aventitous roots by some naturalists) and come to resemble a small sabal palm. The saw palmetto is most easily distinguished from the cabbage or sabal palm by the small, sharp spikes on both sides of the petiole (the branch that holds the fan).

Edible, but not too tasty, palmetto berries are eaten by bears when there's not much else available and have been known to provide nourishment for hungry humans. Despite their limited appeal in the past, these berries have suddenly become highly prized because they are considered an aphrodisiac in the Orient. Extracts of the berries are also marketed as an aid in prostate treatment. Prices for the black berries soared to nearly four dollars a pound in the fall of 1995 and the lowly saw palmetto berry became a cash crop for some residents of Okeechobeeland. At least four people lost their lives picking palmetto berries in 1995 as a result of rattlesnake bites.

(Rattlesnake bites are seldom fatal if early treatment is sought; however, many illegal aliens in the Okeechobee area who harvest palmetto berries are reluctant to seek help for fear of deportation.) These snakes are commonly found in palmetto plants, especially in the wet season when they seek a high place off the ground.

Spanish moss (*Tillandsia usneoides*): The dangling Spanish moss that drapes so many trees in the Lake Okeechobee area does not harm the trees, according to plant experts. Botanists claim the moss, which is not a parasite but a plant living off nutrients in the air, actually benefits the host tree by holding moisture and thus helps the tree through prolonged droughts. It's easy to see that Spanish moss is an air plant by its abundance on sterile utility wires.

On tree trunks and larger branches there may be three- to twelve-inch clumps of a similar plant, often mistaken for Spanish moss. It is wild pine (*Tillandsia setacea*), sometimes called false pine. Its spike of reddish-purple flowers is no longer than its long, slender leaves.

Also growing in the trees and on wires are clumps of plants which look a bit like spiny sea urchins. These may be air plants (*Tillandsia pruinosa*), species of flowering bromeliad (*Bromeliaceae*), or orchids (*Orchidaceae*).

Many other native trees and plants grow in the Lake Okeechobee area, including southern magnolia (*Magnolia grandiflora*), sweetbay (*Magnolia virginiana*), Florida strangler fig (*Ficus aurea*), and red maple (*Acer rubrum*). It's a great place for someone with an interest in botany.

Just as Florida attracts human travelers and tourists, it has also become a naturalized home for exotic plants and trees. The seeds of some of these have arrived, undigested, in the droppings of migrating birds. Others have come ashore on flotsam from the sea, often from Caribbean islands. Still others have been deliberately introduced. Following are some of the exotics most commonly seen in the Lake Okeechobee area:

Brazilian pepper (*Schinus terebinthifolius*): This small tree is sometimes called Florida holly for the abundant red berries it produces. It is an exotic import and a terrible pest. Typically lining both sides of roads, the Brazilian pepper can be easily identified by its green leaves, low stature (usually less than fifteen feet high), and red berries that are especially numerous in the fall and winter. Some birds eat the berries and, consequently, spread the seed far and wide, often flying in a drunken stupor after eating fermented berries.

Once it becomes established, the Brazilian pepper creates a dense monoculture, squeezing out nearly everything else. It has no known natural enemies and, consequently, has spread rapidly in central and southern Florida. Over 200,000 acres of the western Everglades National Park have been taken over by Brazilian pepper. Eradication has been deemed next to impossible by the park management.

Beekeepers are rumored to favor the Brazilian pepper for its superior honey-making characteristics and, perhaps, have helped to propagate its spread. Bees provide a small industry around the Lake Okeechobee area, and commerical hives are common along the Hoover Dike, many in areas of abundant Brazilian pepper trees.

Casuarina or horsetail casuarina (*Casuarina equisetifolia*): An Australian import, it is abundant around Lake Okeechobee. Although it certainly looks like one to the casual observer, this so-called Australian pine is not a true pine tree. What appear to be long needles on these trees are actually tight branchlets. The tree spreads quickly, also creating monocultures to the exclusion of native trees. Few plants can compete for sunlight under this tree or grow in the thick carpet formed by its falling branchlets. It can make effective windbreaks and, for this reason, has been intentionally planted in some places.

Melaleuca (*Melaleuca quinquenervia*): This tree, with its melodic sounding name, deserves special mention because it is considered to be one of the most threatening and environmentally dangerous trees in Florida. Also called the cajeput tree, Australian melaleuca, or punk tree, it is a member of the myrtle family and another exotic from Australia, worse than the pesky Brazilian pepper or casuarina. The melaleuca is best identified by its whitish-brownish peeling bark. It can soak up huge quantities of water and cause considerable damage in wetlands areas. In past years, when the goal was to drain the swamps and dry up the wetlands, this tree was imported to help achieve that end. It was even spread by aerial seeding. Now said to be advancing at the rate of fifty acres per day in the Everglades, it is sometimes referred to as the Everglades terminator. Helicopters and poisons are being used in the battle against this invader. The west and south sides of Lake Okeechobee inside the Hoover Dike are literally blanketed with melaleuca. A line of dead melaleuca can be seen along the northwestern shore of Lake Okeechobee, where an experimental eradication program is in progress. Unlike the Brazilian pepper or the casuarina, which have some beneficial uses, it's difficult to find anything good about melaleuca except that, when chipped, it makes a good mulch, and oil from the tree is sometimes used in shampoos.

Brazilian elodea (*Egeria densa*): Water pest Brazilian elodea is an aquatic perennial from Brazil that has become naturalized in clear springs and streams of Florida and much of the southeastern United States. Its white flower is borne just above the surface on a short stem. Elodea, whose leaves are smooth to the touch, is often given the common name hydrilla, which belongs to its native cousin, the smaller, rough-leafed Florida elodea, *Hydrilla verticillata*. The Brazilian species invaded Florida's waterways many years ago and has grown profusely, choking the streams and lakes, including Lake Okeechobee. Currently, herbicides are used to control its proliferation.

Boaters are asked to carefully wash all traces of hydrilla from their boats when taking them out of the water. Pieces of hydrilla can dry out and appear dead but come back to life when they are in water again. Boaters can thus easily transfer this pest from one body of water to another. And once it gets started, watch out! Hydrilla can easily grow an inch a day.

Water hyacinth (*Eichhornia crassipes*): This beautiful flowering water plant was first displayed in the United States at the Japanese Pavilion during the New Orleans Exposition in 1884. A Florida woman thought its purple blooms would look nice in her fish pond so she brought it to her home on the St. Johns River. She did not realize the water hyacinth would soon become one of the state's worst exotic pests. It escaped her fish pond, reached the St. Johns River, and spread so rapidly that it now chokes canals, streams, lakes, and rivers over the entire state.

This plant is controlled with herbicides. Water hyacinth makes good cattle feed and organic fertilizer, but it is not cost-effective to harvest and process. Cows love them, but since the plants are more than 95 percent water, it is said that a cow can starve to death eating them unless the hyacinths are dried first. Water hyacinth reached Lake Okeechobee in 1897 and has caused considerable problems since then. Lawrence Will, the late Glades historian from Belle Glade, reported the plant grew so thick in places in the water that it could be walked upon.

There are two schools of thought regarding the proliferation of exotics in southern Florida. Some naturalists say it is best to let nature run its course, so the strongest and most adaptable will survive. The majority of naturalists, however, believe that exotics should be kept out and those already established should be eliminated. There is no question that introduced species threaten native species. Often, the newly arrived exotic has no natural enemies in its adopted land and can quickly establish monocultures that crowd out everything else. Most scientists think that if Mother Nature doesn't come up with an enemy for the melaleuca tree soon, and if its spread is not controlled, the Everglades as we know them will disappear.

8 Fauna

*T*he fauna of the Lake Okeechobee area is truly remark-able. Numerous fishes, snakes, turtles, alligators, and mammals are found. Second only to fishes in number, bird life is Okeechobee's chief wildlife attraction for most visitors.

The variety and numbers of birds around Lake Okeechobee are impressive. Some are unique to this area. For, example, other than in Mexico and the southwestern United States, the caracara (Mexican eagle or Mexican buzzard) is found only in southern Florida.

The cane fields of the south are not particularly good places to observe birds except at harvesting time, when great flocks of cattle egrets follow workers and machines to seek dislodged insects. Black vultures, turkey vultures, caracaras, and gulls congregate to feast on small animals killed by cane fires. In contrast to the cane fields, parts of the west and north sides of Lake Okeechobee provide excellent birding year round.

In 1938, the Audubon Society, wanting to save the depleted bird population of Lake Okeechobee, leased a huge part of the marshy western side of the lake from the state. This area remains today under lease to the Audubon Society. It is an idyllic setting of 28,500 acres containing the rookeries of many species of birds. The rookeries are protected and may not be entered during nesting times.

To become more informed about the birds of Lake Okeechobee, visit the local library to look at bird books or buy a bird book and binoculars. Most fishing guides are knowledgeable about the flora and fauna of the lake area, and a guided fishing trip is usually a great learning experience.

Another means of becoming acquainted with the bird life and local nature is to take a trip through the Audubon Reserve. Located at the mouth of the Kissimmee River adjacent to Okee-Tantie Recreation Area (near Okeechobee), Swampland Tours offers a two-hour nature tour in the comfort of a forty-four passenger pontoon boat.

SWAMPLAND TOURS

Swampland tours is operated by Barry "Chop" Lege, a capable third-generation Audubon warden from Louisiana. Highly enthusiastic and dedicated to his work, Lege provides passengers with bird lists so they can check off the birds seen on the tour. He will send this list free to anyone who requests it. Contact Swampland Tours, Kissimmee River Bridge, 10375 Highway 78 West, Okeechobee, FL 34974, (941) 467-4411. Include a self-addressed, stamped envelope with the request.

NORTH SIDE Audubon Warden Barry "Chop" Lege
of Swampland Tours

To discuss all the birds of the Lake Okeechobee area is beyond the scope of this guidebook, but to give newcomers a head start, here are a few:

Pelicans (Family *Pelecanidae*): Both the American white pelican and the brown pelican are found at times in the Lake Okeechobee area. Neither, however, are present here in great numbers as they are in some coastal areas.

American white pelican (*Pelecanus erythrorhynchos*): The white pelican, the second largest bird in North America, migrates across Florida, coming from the far northern states in the fall on its way to the Everglades. White pelicans nearly always can be seen in the winter at Flamingo in Everglades National Park. They are occasionally observed on Lake Okeechobee when they stop for a rest or, more rarely, for an extended visit. Whites hunt by forming a group to herd fish toward shore, where the birds scoop them up in their pouches.

Brown pelican (*Pelecamus occidentalis*): The brown pelican is not seen in great numbers in the Lake Okeechobee area, although a few do make it their home. Unlike the white pelican, the brown loves to dive for its meals. It's exciting to watch these pterodactyl-looking creatures soaring about thirty feet over the water and suddenly plunging head first at full speed into the water after a fish.

WEST SIDE A flock of white pelicans, North America's second largest bird
Photo courtesy of South Florida Water Management District

NORTH SIDE   Female anhinga drying her wings, Taylor Creek

Anhinga (*Anhinga anhinga*): The darter, snake bird, or water turkey is similar to the cormorant in its lack of the water-proofing oils found in most waterfowl. After diving into the water in pursuit of a fish, the anhinga flies to a nearby perch and spreads its wings to dry. Anhingas are dark brown or black birds, up to about thirty six-inches long, with silvery white spots and streaks on their wings and upper back. The female anhinga has a light brown chest and neck features while the male's are dark.

Often mistaken for a cormorant, which is also an abundant species in the Lake Okeechobee area, the anhinga has a sharply pointed beak while the cormorant's is hooked at the end. The anhinga has a longer neck which it is forever turning and poking about; hence, the name darter. When swimming, an anhinga may raise only its head and neck above water and then it may resemble a water snake. The fanning of its tail feathers is responsible for its nickname water turkey. Anhingas spear fish with their daggerlike beaks, toss the fish into the air, and swallow them head first. The large size of fish that both cormorants and anhingas are capable of swallowing is truly

NORTH SIDE   Great blue heron
Photo courtesy of South Florida Water Management District

amazing. Anhingas prefer freshwater habitats like the marshes around the west side of Lake Okeechobee.

The scientific genus and species names for the anhinga are easy to remember — *Anhinga anhinga*.

Herons (Family *Ardeidae*): Several members of the heron family are found in the Lake Okeechobee area. Following are discussions of the cattle egret, snowy egret, great egret, and great blue heron, the heron family members most frequently observed at Lake Okeechobee:

Cattle egret (*Bubulcus ibis*): This adaptable little egret at seventeen inches tall is the smallest (but most widely dispersed) member of the heron family in the Western Hemisphere. The cattle egret, originally an African bird, has established itself, by means of only its own wing power, on six continents. Cattle egrets were unknown in the Western Hemisphere until early in this century when a flock is believed to have flown across the Atlantic Ocean to South America, aided by unusually high winds. These immigrants gradually spread northward, reaching Florida in the 1940s. The first recording of cattle egrets in the United States was at Clewiston in 1941.

The cattle egret is best described as a stubby version of the great egret (see great egret below), with a smaller yellow beak and shorter black legs. They are all white except during breeding season, when they display prominent brownish spots.

This little member of the heron family is quite capable of fishing like its bigger relatives, but it would rather follow animals or machinery around a field. It is easier to feed on insects that have been unearthed or disturbed by grazing and mechanical work. The cattle egret does a great deal of good in controlling insects in the farmlands. Very abundant around Lake Okeechobee, cattle egrets are colonial feeders, i.e., they feed in flocks. They can be seen hanging around cattle herds and, occasionally, one is spotted standing on a cow's back.

The Audubon Society cites the cattle egret as an example of a species undergoing a population explosion when it invades a new area where there are no natural enemies. The cattle egret's numbers have certainly exploded in the Lake Okeechobee area.

Evolutionists talk about niches in nature and of a species evolving or moving in from somewhere else to take advantage of a niche. With all those stirred-up insects, it seems that the cultivated and grazed fields of the Americas were a niche opportunity waiting to be filled, and the cattle egret is taking advantage of it.

Snowy egret (*Egretta thula*): The snowy egret, larger than the cattle egret but smaller than the great egret, can be identified by its size, black beak, and yellow feet. The snowy is called yellow slippers by natives of Florida.

Egrets were hunted nearly to extinction in Florida around the turn of the century because the millinery industry created such a demand for their plumes (aigrettes). Contrary to popular belief, aigrettes are not tail feathers but, rather, back and neck plumes that emerge during breeding season as a sexual attractant. Unfortunately, hunters raided the rookeries where the birds congregated and the adults were slain, leaving young nestlings to die. At one point during this fashion craze, aigrettes were literally worth more than their weight in gold. The snowy egret has the most beautiful nuptial feathers (breeding plumage or aigrettes) of all the birds and was the one most sought after by plume hunters.

Birds of this feather do not always like to flock together, at least during daylight feeding times. They have their own hunting territory staked out and, although

NORTH SIDE Snowy egret, "yellow slippers"
Photo courtesy of South Florida Water Management District

they may tolerate other species, when one of their own trespasses, there is usually a squabble. In the evenings, however, it's a different story. After hunting all day on their own, snowy egrets like to congregate with their clan and head for the roosting spot. In the morning, they head out together again and peel off to their separate stations. Their behavior reminds one of humans carpooling to work.

Unlike the great egret's poised ambush style of fishing, the snowy's feeding technique is to take quick sprints through shallow water to stir up small fish and then quickly peck at its prey.

Great egret (*Casmerodius albus*): The great egret, with white plumage, a yellow bill, and black legs and feet, is the largest of the egrets. A patient bird, it will stand perfectly still in shallow

NORTH SIDE Great blue heron at Taylor Creek

water, beak poised and aimed, waiting to spear an unwary fish. Sometimes called the American egret, this bird, too, was hunted to near extinction by plume hunters. The great egret is another lone territorial hunter but, when the day's work is over, it gathers with its own kind.

Great blue heron (*Ardea herodias*): Slightly larger than the great egret, the great blue heron fishes much the same way, in a poised ambush style. The great blue is the largest of the many species of herons seen around Lake Okeechobee. This bird is readily identified by its blue and gray colors. It also is a territorial hunter. Great blue herons give out a huge squawk occasionally, but no one is sure why.

Some great blue herons may actually be partly or totally white, a color phase. This phenomena, a species having two or more different forms, is known as dimorphism. The white-phased great blues are distinguished from the look-alike great egret by the heron's light-colored legs. The egret's legs are black. The light-colored great blue herons ("great white herons") are usually limited to extreme southern Florida.

Wood stork (*Mycteria americana*): The wood stork, formerly

called the wood ibis, is the only stork found regularly in North America. Another one, the huge jabiru of Central and South America, occasionally roams into south Texas, but it is an infrequent visitor. The wood stork is a true native. In the 1930s, there were tens of thousands in the southern United States. Its numbers declined to less than three thousand nesting pairs in the late 1970s.

Conservationists consider the wood stork an environmental indicator because its decline is linked to people's ongoing damage to the environment. If present trends of development and loss of wetlands continue, it is feared that the wood stork may soon stop breeding in southern Florida.

Wood storks feed by a method known as tacto-location. They wade in the water with their long, stout, slightly curved bill submerged and open. When they feel prey, the bill is snapped shut with the fastest reaction time known for vertebrates. This non-visual feeding method works best where prey is abundant. The wood stork's breeding cycle is based on seasonal drying of wetlands, which concentrates their food supply in small pools. During a single breeding season, a pair of wood storks needs nearly five hundred pounds of food to feed themselves and their brood. Loss of wetlands and unnat-

NORTH SIDE Wood storks on Taylor Creek

ural increases in water levels caused by water management programs can result in disaster for the wood stork. When there is too much water, the food becomes so widely disbursed it is of no value to the stork. If a proper concentration of food is not available, the wood stork simply does not breed.

In spite of its endangered status, the wood stork remains in fairly large numbers in the Lake Okeechobee area. A good place to sight them is along Taylor Creek. Many hang about the banks of the creek at the Zachary Taylor Resort Campground. Wood storks haunt fish cleaning tables looking for handouts, much like brown pelicans do on the seacoasts.

Wood storks are colonial in nature, preferring to feed, roost, and nest with others of their kind. They tend to walk about rather sedately and stand quietly, looking solemn and wise, earning the nickname preacherbird. Other nicknames are ironhead and flinthead. The wood stork's large size, white body, black flight feathers, and dark gray, bare neck and head make them easy to identify.

At the moment, wood storks seem to be making a modest comeback in Florida. Today, it is estimated that there are nearly seven thousand pairs of nesting storks in the state.

White ibis (*Eudocimus albus*): Flocks of white ibis winging their way over Lake Okeechobee in the mornings and evenings are an impressive sight. Called curlews by many natives, they resemble an undulating white ribbon waving across the sky.

The ibis has a slightly downward curving bill which turns red during the breeding season. They were once hunted extensively for food in southern Florida. The species is considered one of special concern, and the Florida Game and Fresh Water Fish Commission wants the white ibis to be designated a threatened species within the state.

Limpkin (*Aramus guarauna*): The limpkin is another species of special concern. Also known as the crying bird, for its eerie night call that sounds like a human in distress, the limpkin is fairly common in the marshlands of western Lake

WEST SIDE Limpkins, the "crying bird," whose principle diet is the apple snail
Photo courtesy of South Florida Water Management District

Okeechobee. Once ranging across Florida, the limpkin owes much of its decline in the state to the fact that it tastes good. The "chicken of the swamp" has also suffered because the apple snail, the limpkin's principal food supply, lives in the wetlands, which are continually shrinking. The limpkin's name comes from its slow, crippled appearance when walking.

THE APPLE SNAIL (*Pomacea paludosa*)

The apple snail deserves special mention. It has been called a water quality indicator because it requires relatively clean water to survive. About the size of a golf ball, it is the largest freshwater snail in North America. It feeds largely on aquatic plant matter but will also eat dead animal tissue. The presence of apple snails is often revealed by their masses of pinkish (immature) to whitish (mature) eggs. They lay their eggs from March through the summer, a few inches above the water line, on almost anything that sticks out of the water. About twenty to thirty eggs are laid in each mass. Incubation takes some twenty days, depending on the temperature. Both sexes are represented in one individual so mating between any two snails is possible. The population of apple snails has been seriously diminished by widespread contamination of fresh-water lakes and streams and the loss of wetlands. This decline has had an impact on the limpkin and the snail kite, since both these birds depend primarily on the apple snail for food. A pile of empty apple snail shells is a good clue that a limpkin or snail kite is in the vicinity.

Limpkins are strange-looking fliers with a rapid upbeat of wings and a slow downward flap.

Common moorhen (*Gallinula chloropus*): Formerly called the common gallinule, this small, beautiful, black bird is abundant in the marshes and on shorelines of Lake Okeechobee and, indeed, the entire state. It is easily identified by a red shield on its forehead.

Black skimmer (*Rynchops niger*): Although most bird books do not indicate the presence of black skimmers on Lake

WEST SIDE Clusters of white apple snail eggs on reeds in Lake Okeechobee. The apple snail is the principal food source for the limpkin and the snail kite (formerly called the Everglades kite). Photo courtesy of South Florida Water Management District

NORTH SIDE Black vultures at Taylor Creek

Okeechobee, they do occur here. Flocks of two or three hundred are seen at times. This splendid bird, the only one on Earth whose lower part of its bill is larger than the upper, skims the surface of the water with its lower bill partly submerged, hoping to snag a fish.

Turkey vulture (*Cathartes aura*): Commonly but inaccurately called turkey buzzards, the turkey vulture is very common in the Lake Okeechobee area in wintertime. Most of them migrate north in the summer. These large birds are readily distinguished from black vultures by their red heads.

Black vulture (*Coragyps atratus*): The black vulture is also very common around Lake Okeechobee in the wintertime. About the same size as the turkey vulture, it is distinguished by its darker head. Like turkey vultures, black vultures feed mostly on carrion. In winter, great flocks of both types of vultures are often seen soaring in circles over potential carrion meals.

Bald eagle (*Haliaeetus leucocephalus*): Florida has more bald eagles than any state except Alaska. The eagle found here is the southern bald eagle, a subspecies slightly smaller than its northern brethren.

Bald eagles mate for life; however, if one dies, the survivor will seek a new partner. Bald eagles are not really bald, but get their name from their white-crowned heads. Young bald eagles have dark heads until they are about five to seven years old, when white feathered crowns and tails develop.

Bald eagles prefer fish, but they also eat small mammals and carrion. Most accidental deaths of bald eagles in Florida occur when they are struck by vehicles while feeding on road-kill.

Although they may be seen occasionally anywhere in the area, the majority of the bald eagles around Lake Okeechobee are found along the marshy west side. There is at least one active nest in the southeastern area near Belle Glade and one or two nests in the Barley Barber Swamp near Indiantown.

Snail kite (*Rostrhamus sociabilis*): Once called the Everglades kite but renamed simply snail kite, this is an endangered species. A few snail kites are found in the western part of Lake Okeechobee. A snail kite is one of the favorite sightings for serious birders. Its principal food is the apple snail.

Osprey (*Pandion haliaetus*): Seen regularly around Lake Okeechobee, the osprey is an expert at catching fish and is especially adapted for this work. Extra-strong muscles in the wings' "wrists" absorb the shock of the bird's headlong plunge onto a fish's back. Long curved talons and rough toe surfaces aid in grasping and holding its catch. Sometimes, in the excitement of the catch, the osprey locks its talons into a fish with such force that it may be unable to let go. Stories have been told about ospreys sinking their talons into too large a fish and being dragged underwater to drown. Fishermen have reportedly caught big fish with dead ospreys attached.

Belted kingfisher (*Ceryle alcyon*): The sassy little belted king-fisher is quite common throughout southern Florida. Able to hover over the water like a helicopter, it carefully sights its prey and then dives for it. The kingfisher normally builds its nest underground along a stream bank. Its back is mostly slate-blue colored and its breast white with stripes. The female's coloration is distinct from the male's. She has two breast stripes, a blue one over a russet one, separated by a white band, while the male has a single blue breast stripe.

Crested caracara (*Caracara plancus audubonii*): The crested caracara is a large bird of prey as unique as the great natural wonder, Lake Okeechobee, around whose shores this feathered beauty makes its home. Florida's caracara has been isolated from the caracara populations of the southwestern United States and Mexico since the Ice Ages eight to ten thousand years ago when rising sea waters from melting glaciers divided its habitat. Today, its distribution in eastern North America is limited to south-central Florida, primarily around Lake Okeechobee and in a few counties to the north.

The national emblem of Mexico, caracaras are also called Mexican eagles or Mexican buzzards. They are not, however, true buzzards, but are closely related to hawks and falcons. Their call is a high, harsh cackle for which they are named. These birds may have the most varied diet of any bird of prey — feeding on insects, small animals, and carrion. Occasionally, they are seen circling with turkey vultures and black vultures. The caracara is a threatened species with only about five hundred nesting pairs remaining in Florida. Most deaths occur when these birds feed on roadkill and are struck by a vehicle. They mate for life and are very territorial, nesting in cabbage palms and other tall trees.

Many other species and subspecies of birds are found in this natural wonderland. Crows, ducks, geese, gulls, killdeers, and red-shouldered hawks are common. The large and beautiful sand hill crane is often seen. Florida's state bird, the mockingbird, also inhabits the Lake Okeechobee area.

The isolated nature of Florida's peninsula has produced several unique species and subspecies, like the aforementioned caracara. Others include the little burrowing owl (found in the uplands, away from the water) and the scrub jay (a threatened species). And the normal distribution of the smooth billed ani, a member of the cuckoo family, is limited to southern Florida.

Besides the remarkable birdlife of Okeechobeeland, there are numerous other interesting animals in the area. They include the following:

American alligator (*Alligator mississippiensis*): The adult alligator, at the top of the food chain in Lake Okeechobee, has no natural enemies except humans. Interestingly, the alligator begins life near the bottom of the food chain. The mortality of alligator hatchlings is estimated to be 80 to 90 percent. Young ones are vulnerable, especially to being eaten by water birds and raccoons. Since their fathers will eat them, too, the safest place for little gators is around their mother. A dozen or more small ones can sometimes be observed sunning themselves on the bank next to her. They may stay close to their mother until they are well over a year old.

Even though feeding alligators is against the law, some people still do it. Feeding alligators creates an extremely dangerous situation because the animals become accustomed to humans and associate them with food. Consequently, when someone later comes close to shore with a small dog or child, tragedy may result.

Nine-banded armadillo (*Dasypus novemcinctus*): The common nine-banded armadillo of Florida is an exotic species. Several of these animals escaped from an overturned circus truck in 1924. A few more gained their independence from another circus in 1936 during a hurricane. The descendants of these fugitives are now plentiful in the Lake Okeechobee area. And armadillos which invaded Texas from Mexico in the 1800s have now extended their range into the Florida Panhandle.

Feral hogs: There are over a half million wild hogs in Florida. None are native to the state. They are descendants of domestic pigs brought in by the Spaniards, English, and later settlers or they are wild boars introduced for hunting. Feral hogs may be hunted on private property at any time of the year without a license (with permission from the landowner).

Because of its extensive rooting and voracious feeding, the hog can cause serious environmental damage. Hunters kill about 10 percent of the feral hog population each year, but the animals are fast breeders with a low mortality rate and they easily replace their losses.

Wild hog hunting is a popular sport in the Lake Okeechobee countryside, particularly in the western and northern areas.

River otter (*Lutra canadensis*): The river otter, once hunted to near extinction for its valuable fur, is again plentiful. This delightful, playful creature is often seen in the Kissimmee River and Fisheating Creek, the two major natural streams flowing into Lake Okeechobee.

Snakes: Florida is one of the few places where varieties of all four of the poisonous snakes of North America can be found. These are the cottonmouth or water moccasin, rattlesnake, coral snake, and copperhead.

Cottonmouth moccasin (*Agkistrodon piscivorus*): The cottonmouth moccasin or water moccasin is found throughout Florida. It has a reputation for aggressiveness, and there are stories told about the moccasin climbing into boats to bite people. These are probably undocumented exaggerations, but it is true that a water moccasin is not always willing to slither off when a person approaches. Instead, it may move only a few feet away and coil with its mouth open, revealing the white lining as a warning. The snake's fangs are relatively short and its bite is seldom fatal to an adult. Moccasins can bite underwater, but the force of their strike is slowed by water resistance. They avoid clear, open water and are not normally a problem to swimmers.

Rattlesnakes: The rattlesnake is more risky to people than the moccasin, and some naturalists consider it to be the most dangerous wild creature in Florida. Usually found in areas drier than the habitat of the water moccasin, the rattlesnake is quite abundant in southern Florida. Two of the species found here are the Eastern diamondback rattlesnake (*Crotalus adamanteus*) and the dusky pygmy rattlesnake (*Sistrurus miliarius barbouri*). The diamondback can grow to an awesome size, some reaching over six feet long.

Coral snake (*Micrurus fulvius*): Even more deadly than rattlesnake venom is that of the native Eastern coral snake. However, these little snakes with cobra-type poison are reclusive, and they rarely present a threat unless they are carelessly handled.

Southern copperhead (*Agkistrodon contortrix*): The Southern copperhead is found only in the Florida Panhandle. However, many residents and visitors to the Lake Okeechobee area believe they have seen copperheads there. The confusion arises from incorrect identification, usually of harmless water snakes or young water moccasins. Although mature water moccasins are typically dark-gray or black, young cottonmouths have yellow and brown patterns that closely resemble those of a copperhead.

Unfortunately, snakes in southern Florida do not hibernate in the cold months, so one must be on the lookout for them year round.

No discussion of the fauna of Lake Okeechobee would be complete without mentioning insects. Sometimes it seems the insects have the upper hand around Lake Okeechobee. There are three groups that pester folks the most:

Mosquitoes: There's no denying it, mosquitoes can be bothersome at times around the lake. They're usually not too annoying out on the water, but they can be a nuisance onshore. Long-sleeved protective clothing and modern repellents provide the best defense. Winter months offer the most relief from mosquitoes.

On rare occasions, mosquitoes have been known to transmit encephalitis from animals to humans.

Fire ants: The fire ant is another exotic now found all over Florida. When their nest is disturbed, these little creatures can attack an unwary victim by the hundreds, causing nasty bites that may be especially dangerous for allergic victims. Their irregularly shaped earthen mounds are easy to recognize. The best defense is vigilance and avoidance. Fire ants do not normally attack a walking person, but one should beware of standing on or near their nest!

No-see-ums: The itching caused by these tiny flying creatures is usually a short-lived effect. Repellents are effective against them.

9 Fishing Lake Okeechobee

It's Friday afternoon. Dr. Blair Snoke, of Seminole, Florida (near St. Petersburg), has just seen his last patient of the day. Towing a Ranger bass boat behind his Chevy Suburban, Dr. Snoke speeds down Interstate 275, his destination the "Big O," Lake Okeechobee. Although he's made this trip countless times, he's as pumped up as a young kid going on a first big fishing trip. "Nothing like it for me," he says. "The excitement of heading out there again and the relaxation of fishing once I'm there never gets old for me. There's nothing better than heading to the lake country on a fishing trip."

Snoke, a transplanted Ohioan who has lived and practiced dentistry in Seminole for years, has an office and home within a mile of the beautiful Gulf of Mexico. Yet he shuns ocean fishing. "It's not for me. I get tired of getting pounded to death out there by the waves and fighting rust from the salt water. I'll take freshwater fishing anytime. The sheer joy of hooking and landing a big Florida black bass is as exhilarating as catching anything the sea has to offer. And I thoroughly enjoy the nature out there. The alligators, the otters, the bird life — they all fascinate me. I don't get to see that out on the Gulf. Even if I don't catch anything, which rarely happens, I still feel like I got my money's worth."

Dr. Snoke's not the only one who gets a thrill out of heading to the Big O. The big lake attracts anglers from around the world. And they come back time and time again.

Steve Gormak, a biologist for the Florida Game and Fresh Water Fish Commission who monitors Lake Okeechobee's fish from spawning to adult size, says, "This is a fantastic place. There is no place that, day in and day out, can compare with Okeechobee, not only for fish, but for the lake itself; its size, history, and wildlife."

For newcomers, the best way to fish Lake Okeechobee for the first time is with an experienced guide. Most of the larger towns around the lake have local guides, and the chamber of commerce in each town can recommend a good service (see phone numbers in the Introduction). Although the cost can run more than $200 for a half-day fishing trip for two people, it is well worth the expense to get a proper introduction to the lake and to learn how to fish local style.

Of course, one can always bring a boat (or rent one — rentals are readily available around the lake), assemble the necessary fishing gear, and go it alone. It is not, however, the best way to take that initial trip. Several launch sites require passage through a lock to get to Lake Okeechobee. Going through a lock with a boat can be a rather harrowing experience. It is more comfortable to do this the first time with an experienced guide.

The day starts early on Lake Okeechobee. Before first light, boats are buzzing like bees from boat ramps and locks around the lake. The morning shift usually runs from just before daylight to about 11:30 A.M. It's one of the busiest times on the lake, especially during the warmer months. The slick bass boats travel fast, some up to fifty miles per hour, in their hurry to get to the choice fishing grounds.

Okeechobee's big bass are one of the most sought-after game fish in the world. Southern Florida's black bass are an isolated strain of largemouth with an unusually high growth rate and a scrappy nature. Within a year of birth, these bass reach a length of eight to ten inches and weigh half a pound. The popularity of bass fishing is indicated by the estimated

NORTH SIDE   Locking through Taylor Creek to head for a day of speck fishing   Photo courtesy of South Florida Water Management District

ten thousand bass tournaments held yearly in the state, a large percentage of them on Lake Okeechobee, where the biggest fish consistently are caught. Nearly a million people enjoy this competitive sport each year in Florida. Appropriately, the black bass is the state's official freshwater fish.

The bait of choice for the prized bass is wild shiners. These fish are caught in Lake Okeechobee and other areas, sold for about a dollar apiece, and kept in aerated containers or in wells in the boats. Some shiners are over six inches long, almost a meal in themselves. Domestic shiners are smaller and cheaper, but the wild ones make better bait because they are more active in the water and attract the attention of bass. The domestics have not been exposed to predators and show less fear of bass, so they are not as apt to dart away and lead the bass to give chase. Some of the more experienced bass anglers on Lake Okeechobee go top-water fishing with assorted lures.

The guides and old-timers seek out the edges of tussocks, floating masses of sea lettuce, water hyacinths, and other grassy weeds which provide fish shelter from aerial hunters.

They cast the shiners or lures along the edges of these weed islands, hoping to entice a big bass to dart out from under its protective cover and grab the bait. When the bass are hitting, there's nothing quite like the action on Lake Okeechobee. The bass are fierce fighters that thrash and break the water in their attempts to throw off the hook. Guides may also look for a drop-off where bass, hiding in adjacent thick hydrilla, often dart out of their hiding place to grab the bait.

Experienced anglers usually use short, stiff rods with twenty-pound monofilament line and a shiner hooked through both lips. Attached to a slack line is a bobber float with the bait set at two or three feet. When the bass hits, the angler slowly takes up the slack in the line and then gives it a hard, fast yank straight up and back toward the face to set the hook. The line is reeled in as quickly as possible. Give it any slack and the bass will be long gone.

Bass can range over ten pounds (the confirmed record for Florida's black bass is 17.27 pounds; the uncertified record is 20.13 pounds) with a huge mouth that will easily hold a person's fist. Generally, any bass over four pounds is female.

WEST SIDE   Bass fishing alongside a "tussock," a floating island of vegetation   Photo courtesy of South Florida Water Management District

Almost everyone practices catch and release by returning large bass to the lake for breeding. The tournaments return over 95 percent of their catches alive.

The shiner might be attacked by a pickerel or a big gar, the latter sometimes over one hundred pounds. The guides, however, are usually after black bass. Yet there are some forty species of fish in Lake Okeechobee, and bass are not the only fishes that are highly prized. Catfish are a delicacy and are avidly sought by some who claim their firm flesh is far superior to that of farm-raised catfish.

For every person fishing for bass or catfish on Lake Okeechobee there must be at least a dozen who are after speckled perch (except, perhaps, in the warmer months). Nothing compares to perch for just plain good eating. Anywhere else in the country these are called black crappie, but in Lake Okeechobee they are "specks." More than two million of these fish are pulled from the lake each year while hundreds of thousands more are released as too small.

The vehicle of choice for many speckled perch anglers is a pontoon boat, rigged with comfortable seating and multiple cane poles. It's not unusual to see a pontoon boat with ten

NORTH SIDE Fishing for specks

cane poles extending from each side of the deck. Some of these boats carry TVs and have comfort facilities. Many boats are rigged with lights for night fishing. On some nights during the fall, winter, and spring, there are "cities of light" out on the lake.

The usual bait for specks is small minnows, called Missouri minnows. In warm weather, fishing is best in the deepest, coldest holes, so the lines are rigged to keep the bait a foot or so off the bottom. As the waters cool, the specks move into shallower water and closer to shore. Some anglers practice drift fishing while searching for the good holes. The current limit on specks is fifty per person per day. Electric filleting knives are the easiest and fastest way to clean these fish.

Snook and other large fish usually associated with coastal fishing are often caught, particularly in the Caloosahatchee River near the Moore Haven Lock and in the St. Lucie Canal near the Port Mayaca Lock. Alien fishes, like tarpon, are sometimes caught on the Big O. While Lake Okeechobee has no natural connection to the sea, dredging and canalizing has allowed tarpon and several other exotic species to invade these waters.

It's usually delightful on the lake in the mornings. Birds are awakening from their major nesting grounds, and flocks head out for the day's work. Ribbons of curlews (white ibis) wend their way across the sky along with great flocks of cattle egrets and others. Invariably, the anglers will attract a great blue heron, some great egrets, and gulls which hang around the anchored boat, hoping for an easy meal of a cast-off shiner.

Although a boat is helpful to fish Lake Okeechobee, it is not a necessity. There are places all around the lake where the fishing is good from the shore — the fishing pier at Jaycee Park in Okeechobee, the Nubbin Slough Floodgates area, and the Pahokee Town Park Pier are a few. On weekends, there are large crowds at Port Mayaca, where fishing is intense in the St. Lucie Canal adjacent to the lock. Nearly all the canals around the lake are popular fishing spots.

WEST SIDE Airboat operating in the west side marshes of Lake Okeechobee   Photo courtesy of South Florida Water Management District

Airboats are also used on the lake. These speedy craft draw little water and enable hunters and fishers to reach otherwise inaccessible spots.

For those angling from shore or for from a boat, fishing the Big O is a special treat. It's a unique spot, as exciting a place as anywhere on Earth to spend some fishing time. Just ask Dr. Snoke.

10 Florida National Scenic Trail

For decades after the construction of the massive Herbert Hoover Dike, the U.S. Army Corps of Engineers and other authorities zealously guarded the structure. A primitive road traversed the top of the levee for nearly 110 miles around the lake, but only authorized personnel and vehicles were allowed to travel this route. Locked gates and no trespassing signs kept the public off the dike. Then, in 1993, through the

WEST SIDE Nubbin Slough. The Herbert Hoover Dike and Lake Okeechobee are in the foreground. The small community of Upthegrove Beach is to the right. Photo courtesy of South Florida Water Management District

BIKE AND HIKE TOURS

Biking and hiking tours of the Lake Okeechobee area are offered by various organizations. Okeechobee Cyclists is a non-profit group that meets regularly on Saturdays for bicycle rides on the Herbert Hoover Dike through the Brighton Indian Reservation and on other interesting trails. Okeechobee Outback Tours, Route 2, Box 430, Lakeport, Florida 33471, (941) 946-3228, offers one-day rides, weekend rides, and custom tours. Shi-High Lake Adventures, 16 River Road, Moore Haven, Florida 33471, (941) 946-2075, is another. Euler's Cycle and Fitness on U.S. Route 441/State Route 78 in Okeechobee, (941) 357-0458, rents bicycles and has information on tours.

efforts of the Florida Trail Association and others, Congress certified the Florida National Scenic Trail which passes through the Lake Okeechobee area. One of only eight National Scenic Trails, this passage will eventually meander for hundreds of miles from the Florida Panhandle to Big Cypress National Preserve. The Okeechobee segment of the Florida Trail consists of four contiguous parts along the top of the Hoover Dike. The high structure offers a panoramic view of the lake, the countryside, and the local flora and fauna.

Today, visitors are welcome to travel the trail on foot or by bicycle, and increasing numbers are doing so each year. Several groups sponsor tours.

Hiking and biking groups hold events around Lake Okeechobee yearly, usually in the cooler months of the year. Participants of all ages are encouraged to join.

The top of the dike can be accessed at more than twenty-four sites around the lake. All towns on the lakefront have nearby points where the dike road can be reached.

Numerous primitive campsites along the Hoover Dike are marked by symbols of the Florida Trail Association and improved campsites are available at many RV resorts. Hotels are close to the dike in Okeechobee, South Bay, Clewiston, Moore Haven, and Lakeport.

Plans are underway to improve the Hoover Dike Trail. An ambitious program will eventually lead to a paved road on top of the dike for pedestrians, bicyclists, skaters, and others. Alongside the dike, but off the crest, an equestrian trail is planned, and other amenities are foreseen by some. The Florida Department of Transportation has initiated a master plan for the Okeechobee segment of the Florida National Scenic Trail which, when completed, could make this area one of the top recreational destinations in the world.

11 The North Side of Lake Okeechobee

*T*he north side of Lake Okeechobee differs from the rest of the area. There were no significant wetlands here to drain for rich muck lands. Consequently, farming was never extensive in this sector. However, the land was ideal for pasture, and cattle became the important industry.

Okeechobee County is the predominant geographical/political entity of the northern area. Extending northward from the lake for approximately thirty-two miles, this county includes about twenty-one miles of the north Lake Okeechobee shoreline. Its beef and dairy farming enterprises are the largest in the state.

Some of Okeechobee County's beef cattle and other ranches offer interesting tours. Cooper's Dark Hammock Ranch is in an idyllic setting and luncheons can be arranged for visitors. A visit here offers an excellent opportunity to view native flora and fauna. Deer, feral pigs, and other wildlife can be seen at Dark Hammock Ranch.

Events related to cows or horses take place year-round in the Okeechobee County area. It may be the Great Florida Trail Drive from Yeehaw Junction (just north of Okeechobee County) to Kissimmee, or a horse show or rodeo. The latter events are held at the Okeechobee Cattlemen's Association Arena in Okeechobee and at the nearby Brighton Indian Reservation.

LARSEN DAIRY FARM

The largest dairy farm in Okeechobee County and surely one of the largest in the world is Larsen Dairy Farm, located about fifteen miles north of Okeechobee. With an astonishing herd size of about ten thousand cows (over one-fourth of the total dairy cattle in Okeechobee County), milk production is handled in a scientific manner. Nutrient runoff is closely monitored and controlled to reduce potential pollution of Lake Okeechobee. Larsen Dairy Farm encourages tours. To obtain additional information, or to arrange a tour, call the Okeechobee Chamber of Commerce at (941) 763-6464 or (800) 871-4403.

NORTH SIDE Larsen Dairy Farm

Tourism is Okeechobee County's second largest industry (after cattle). At times in the winter months, the thirty five thousand year-long residents of Okeechobee County seem to be outnumbered by snowbirds and other visitors.

In addition to the city of Okeechobee, some other communities on the north side are Upthegrove Beach, historic Fort Basinger/Basinger, and Fort Drum. The latter two were army forts dating from the Seminole Indian Wars. Fort Basinger was established by Colonel Zachary Taylor a few days before his fight with the Seminoles at the Battle of Okeechobee on Christmas Day, 1837.

Okeechobee

Okeechobee is unique, totally different from any other town or city in Florida. Basically, Okeechobee is a large cow town, full of cowboy hats and pickup trucks. It caters to the needs of the dairy and cattle ranches of Okeechobee County and nearby areas. Okeechobee was established in pioneer days when the first settlers came here looking for additional grazing lands for their cattle. It remains a cattle-oriented town today. There are other Florida cow towns, to be sure, but Okeechobee has the Okeechobee Livestock Market, the largest cattle market in the state (and the second largest east of the Mississippi River). Moreover, no other similar town is situated at such a natural wonder as Lake Okeechobee.

Okeechobee City, or simply Okeechobee, calls itself the "Gateway to Southern Florida," or "Florida's Dairy Capital." With approximately forty-eight hundred year-round residents, the incorporated city encompasses about four and a half square miles located three miles north of the lakeshore, centering at the intersection of east-west State Route 70 (Park Street) and north-south U.S. Route 441 (Parrott Avenue). It is a center of activity.

The greater Okeechobee City area includes a large region of houses, trailer camps, and shopping centers extending for several miles on either side of the Route 70/Route 441 inter-

OKEECHOBEE LIVESTOCK MARKET

The Cattlemen's Association operates the Okeechobee Livestock Market, where sales are held every Monday and Tuesday. The public is welcome. Cattle are brought individually into a small arena and sold. The auctioneer, bookkeepers, bidders, and visitors overlook the arena. Comfortable spectator seating is provided and there is no admission charge. The market is located on State Route 98 just a mile and a half from the center of Okeechobee. A visit to the cattle market on auction day is an interesting experience.

section. An Okeechobee mailing address could be anywhere in Okeechobee County plus some of the neighboring communities. The Okeechobee Post Office is quite large, occupying about half a block on east Park Street.

The first white settlers, the Peter and Louisiana Raulerson family, arrived in 1896 and took up residence along a bend in Taylor Creek, three miles north of the Lake Okeechobee shoreline and about a half mile east of the present-day center of Okeechobee. More settlers soon arrived and a small, thriving community began.

Originally named Tantie after one of the first schoolteachers here, Tantie Huckabee, the new settlement became known as a wild and woolly frontier town in its early days. Hunters, catfishers, loggers, and cowboys came here to relax, drink, and fight on weekends.

Tantie, renamed Okeechobee in 1912, was incorporated in 1915 when the railroad arrived. When "Fingey" Connors built his new toll road from the east coast to Okeechobee in 1924, residents had dreams of greatness for this town. Okeechobee could become the "Chicago of the South." The great city of Chicago was on the shore of the largest freshwater lake within the confines of the United States; Okeechobee was on the shore of the largest freshwater lake outside of the Great Lakes.

Much of Okeechobee's colorful early history can be reviewed at the Okeechobee Historical Museum. A vintage home, the Freedman Raulerson House, can be visited.

OKEECHOBEE HISTORICAL MUSEUM

The Okeechobee Historical Museum is in Okeechobee Historical Park, just northwest of Okeechobee on State Route 98 (northwest of the cattle market). This little museum contains many exhibits from the early days, including the original wood-frame schoolhouse built in 1909. Old newspapers and other documents are available for perusal. The museum is open only on Thursdays from 9 A.M. to 1 P.M.

FREEDMAN RAULERSON HOUSE

Now on the National Register of Historic Places, this house was built in 1932. Freedman Raulerson was the son of Peter and Louisiana Raulerson who, in 1896, became the first settlers at Okeechobee. The house is on 2nd Avenue just north of 4th Street.

Okeechobee never became the Chicago of the South nor did it replace Tallahassee as Florida's capital city, as some of its early residents had hoped, but it still is an interesting place. It is a city with a wealth of community pride, an excellent school system, and a high level of interest in its young people, in keeping with the tradition set by Pogey Bill. In addition, it has a low crime rate, numerous churches, uncrowded streets, and friendly folks. Fund-raising benefits for those who have suffered a tragedy are common. Visitors are often startled by strangers saying "Hi!" on the street. The politeness of the natives is a welcome surprise to many visitors from the north. "Yes sir," "No sir," "Yes ma'am," "No ma'am," are a natural part of the language of Okeechobeeans.

Upon entering Okeechobee today, one's first impression is that it's clean and neat with spacious, well-designed streets. The layout of the town is no accident. It was planned under the supervision of the Florida East Coast Railroad, Henry Flagler's line. Flagler was the tycoon who brought the railroads to east Florida, including the line to Okeechobee.

NORTH SIDE   White ibis along the Kissimmee River. Called "curlews" by many natives, the white ibis has a distinctive long curved beak which turns red during the breeding season.

Photo courtesy of South Florida Water Management District

NORTH SIDE   The Kissimmee River, the principle stream that flows into Lake Okeechobee, where it enters the lake. The Okee-Tantie Marina and Campground are to the left. The small community of Buckhead Ridge is to the right.   Photo courtesy of South Florida Water Management District

SOUTH SIDE   The historic swing bridge over the Okeechobee Waterway to the Belle Glade Campground on Torry Island
Photo courtesy of South Florida Water Management District

WEST SIDE   "Chickee" hut at the Brighton Seminole Indian Reservation
Photo courtesy of South Florida Water Management District

SOUTH SIDE   The Kissimmee Billie Swamp Safari area at the Big Cypress
Seminole Indian Reservation
Photo courtesy of South Florida Water Management District

WEST SIDE   The famous lone cypress tree at Moore Haven that was used for decades as a navigation marker by boaters on Lake Okeechobee.   Photo courtesy of South Florida Water Management District

EAST SIDE   Port Mayaca Cemetery. The plaque beneath the flag honors 1,800 victims of the 1928 hurricane who are buried here in a mass grave.   Photo courtesy of South Florida Water Management District

EAST SIDE   Lock at Port Mayaca on the Okeechobee Waterway
Photo courtesy of South Florida Water Management District

WEST SIDE   Cypress Kneeland, Palmdale

NORTH SIDE   Lake Okeechobee's north shore

EAST SIDE   Aerial photograph looking north along Herbert Hoover Dike in the Pahokee area. The town of Pahokee is to the right and the Pahokee Marina and Campground is to the left. U.S. Sugar's giant Bryant Mill Sugar Refinery can be seen in distant right.
Photograph by Tim Christopher

NORTH SIDE   Rodeo at Brighton Seminole Indian Reservation

NORTH SIDE   Sunset over Lake Okeechobee from Nubbin Slough
Photo courtesy of South Florida Water Management District

Lodging

There are a number of comfortable places to stay in the greater Okeechobee area. A complete list of facilities as well as dining places and other information can be obtained from the Okeechobee Chamber of Commerce.

Holiday Inn (on South Parrott Avenue, opened in 1996), Flamingo Hotel (next door to the Holiday Inn), Motel Pier II/Day's Inn (on U.S. Route 441/State Route 98 along the rim canal adjacent to Lake Okeechobee), and Wanta Linga (on U.S. Route 441/State Route 98) offer some of the best accommodations.

There is an abundance of RV parks and fishing camps in the Okeechobee area, nearly all of which are very neat and clean. Many of these parks offer cabins or other facilities for overnight lodging. The KOA Campground on South Parrott Avenue is the largest KOA in North America. In addition to its 756 RV and tent sites, it has ten air-conditioned cabins for rent. The Zachary Taylor Resort on U.S. Route 441 is at an idyllic setting along the east bank of beautiful Taylor Creek. Here one can tie up a boat and, when the urge arises, take the craft through the Taylor Creek Lock into Lake Okeechobee in minutes. Ancient Oaks, farther down U.S. Route 441 at Upthegrove Beach, is another highly rated campground in the Okeechobee area. All of these camps offer numerous activities for residents.

One should not overlook the smaller and less-well-known motels, hotels, campgrounds, and fishing camps — some of which offer quality lodging at very reasonable prices.

The Okee-Tantie Recreation Area, about four miles west of Okeechobee on State Route 70, is one of the very few campgrounds directly on the Lake Okeechobee waterfront. Actually, it is on the bank of the Kissimmee River, but one can launch a boat here, head down the river a short distance, and, without passing through a lock, be out on the great lake in a few minutes.

There are no restrictions on the length of time one can stay at this beautiful RV and tent campground, which is owned and operated by the county. The park contains a marina, multiple boat ramps, a bait and tackle shop, picnic areas, and Lightsey's Seafood Restaurant. There are several places here where one can fish in the river.

Dining

The Newcomer and Tourist Guide (available from the Okeechobee Chamber of Commerce) lists fifty-four restaurants in the greater Okeechobee area. Many of these are standard fast-food franchises, located mostly along Park Street and Parrott Avenue. There is also a state-of-the-art Shoneys restaurant, built in 1994, where the planners had enough foresight to provide for RV parking. Shoneys will soon build a motel to complement the restaurant.

Pogeys is a popular family dining spot. The name comes from "Pogey Bill" Collins, the well-loved character and one-time sheriff of Okeechobee County. Pogeys opens at five in the morning to cater to the early fishing crowd. Breakfast is served all day. Michael's, on Parrott Street, is another popular dining spot. Captain Earl's is a seafood restaurant on Park Street.

A short distance east of Parrott Street, along U.S. Route 441/State Route 98, is the Lakeside Restaurant where the "world-famous" Okeeburger can be ordered. Bring a friend if you order one of these — they're huge! Old Habits, a family eating place, is further east on U.S. Route 441/State Route 98, at the Battle of Okeechobee Monument, about a mile east of Taylor Creek. An unimposing stone marker with a metal plate bearing an inscription marks the approximate place where the Battle of Okeechobee was fought on Christmas Day, 1837, between the Seminoles and Colonel Zachary Taylor's federal troops.

Many of these restaurants serve beer and wine. For cocktails and entertainment with one's meals, there are several other spots to visit in the greater Okeechobee area.

As might be expected in a cow town, the bigger and, arguably, better places to eat and be entertained at are steak houses. Alas, however, the meat most likely came all the way from Omaha, Nebraska. The cattle sold at the Okeechobee Livestock Market are sent north to be fattened. It seems it's cheaper to fatten the cattle near the slaughterhouses than it is to ship grain to Okeechobee and then ship the fattened cattle north. The larger steak houses serve liquor and have bands, usually of the country-western variety.

The Angus is on Park Street, about a mile west of the center of town. It offers karaoke and other entertainment. Brewskis, on U.S. Route 441/State Route 98 just past Taylor Creek, has entertainment and a small dining area. The Brahma Bull on U.S. Route 441/State Route 98 just west of Taylor Creek, offers excellent food and has entertainment.

One of the best-kept culinary secrets in Okeechobee is the Speckled Perch Restaurant, at the intersection of Park Street and State Route 98 on the northwest side of town. Customers can't order specks, however — it's a game fish not legally sold in public restaurants. The Speckled Perch is a favorite steak house and watering hole for locals. Expect to see several ranchers with their Stetsons on dining with their ladies. The dining room is open on Thursday, Friday, and Saturday nights only.

Other Amenities

The greater Okeechobee City area has a large movie theater, some huge flea markets, a bowling alley, an airport with a five-thousand foot runway, a community theater, an industrial park, an Amtrak station, golf courses, bingo halls, and much more.

The Speckled Perch Festival is the major event of the year in Okeechobee. Sponsored by the Cattlemen's Association and the Chamber of Commerce, this gala affair is held in March. The fun includes a parade and rodeo.

Fishing, of course, is a big drawing card at Okeechobee.

Although many prefer to fish out on the lake from a boat, there are many spots around Okeechobee where one can catch fish from shore. Jaycee Park, at the south end of Parrott Avenue, is a favorite spot, as is nearby Nubbin Slough.

The large Jaycee Park (Lock 7) is on the shore of Lake Okeechobee, inside the Hoover Dike. The park has a beach, fishing pier, and a double boat ramp for launching directly into the lake. It also provides a great view of the big lake and is a nice place from which to view a beautiful sunset. Fossils from the underlying bedrock of the Fort Thompson Formation are abundant in the rubble around the park.

Nubbin Slough is a relatively large waterway that feeds through big floodgates into Lake Okeechobee. It is about 4.6 miles east of the end of Parrott Avenue on U.S. Route 441/State Route 98. One can drive over the Hoover Dike into a large parking area where there is a boat ramp for launching directly into Lake Okeechobee. The area around the lake side of the floodgates is a popular fishing spot. This is also a nice place from which to view a sunset.

NORTH SIDE Fishing at Nubbin Slough

HIKING AND BIKING ON THE HOOVER DIKE
At Okeechobee, the top of the Hoover Dike can be reached at Jaycee Park (Lock 7). Going east, it's about two and two-tenths miles from Jaycee Park to the Taylor Creek Lock and it's another two and one-half miles from there to Nubbin Slough. From Jaycee Park it is about four miles southwest along the Hoover Dike to the Okee-Tantie Recreational Area.

There is exotic granite riprap around the south sides of the Nubbin Slough floodgates and local limestone riprap along the lakefront. Watch for water moccasins in the riprap. For some reason, in spite of all the human activity, this is a favorite hangout for cottonmouths. Some fossils can be seen where Fort Thompson limestone debris is exposed in places. The banks of the access road leading into Nubbin Slough are also a good place to view fossils. Comorants are usually plentiful here. Alligators may bask in the sun along the adjacent shorelines, and turtles are abundant in the water around the floodgates, often poking their heads above water.

Weekends in Okeechobee bring large crowds to the Saturday night bingo game at the downtown American Legion Hall. The Saturday night auction at 7 P.M. at the Florida Traders Auction Barn on U.S. Route 441/State Route 98, two and seven-tenths miles east from the south end of Parrott Avenue, always draws another big crowd. During the day on the weekends, the flea markets are in full swing.

For those seeking a little more action, there are abundant bars and pubs in town. For many, however, the real fun is at the campgrounds. At the larger ones, there are card games, dances, craft works, and other activities.

Many visitors who come to Okeechobee like it so much they decide to stay. There are few places in the country with more reasonably priced housing than the greater Okeechobee area. Some prefer to live in an RV at one of the nice campgrounds or in more spacious quarters such as a double wide mobile home. Conventional houses are readily available, some in gorgeous settings.

There are no private lakefront houses on Lake Okeechobee. Many waterfront homes and trailer parks are along inlets such as Taylor Creek, the rim canal adjacent to the big lake, and on other connecting canals. Here, one can tie up the boat in the backyard and, when ready to fish or cruise, take the craft down the creek or canal, pass through one of the locks and, within minutes, be on Lake Okeechobee.

Upscale developments such as River Oaks, on the bank of the Kissimmee River about eight miles west of town, are also found in the area. At River Oaks, residents have their own private airstrip and most have hangars for planes in their backyards.

If someone is looking for a quiet place, reasonable housing, closeness to nature, social activity, and friendly folks, these can likely be found in the cow town of Okeechobee.

Upthegrove Beach

Other than Okeechobee, Upthegrove Beach is the only community on the north shore of Lake Okeechobee (Buckhead Ridge is included in the western sector). Actually, since Okeechobee lies north of the lake, Upthegrove Beach could be considered the only north shore town.

Upthegrove Beach begins at Nubbin Slough and extends for a few miles east along U.S. Route 441/State Route 98. It is a community of mobile homes, RV resorts, fishing camps, and private homes. The unusual name comes from Robert Upthegrove and his sons and brothers, who were early settlers here.

At one time there was another town called Utopia a few miles down the highway to the east. This was a little fishing village founded in the early 1900s, complete with a school and post office, but when the catfishing industry declined in the 1940s, so did the town and it eventually disappeared.

12 The South Side of Lake Okeechobee

*T*he south side of Lake Okeechobee is as different from the north as night is from day. Where cattle is king on the northern shores of the lake, sugarcane reigns in the south. Before drainage, this was the heart of the northern Everglades, with thick, black muck at the bottom of swampy waters. Muck was ideal for growing vegetables and the tropical plant sugarcane — all that had to be done was drain the water and plant the crops. No fertilizers were needed in those early days for this rich organic soil.

Settlement along the southern shore of Lake Okeechobee occurred later than in the north. Whereas the first settlers began appearing at Okeechobee in the late 1800s, the settlements in the south had to wait for drainage and clearing of custard apple trees and moon vines. By the early 1900s, transformation of the land was in full swing and settlements began to spring up along the lake. Small vegetable farms prospered at times, but the real cash crop became sugarcane. When many of the small vegetable farms failed during hard times because of flood, drought, or freezes, cane became the dominant crop. Sugarcane fields now cover the largest percentage of the old swamplands. Other principal crops grown in the area include tomatoes, lettuce, rice, sweet corn, cucumbers, radishes, peppers, eggplant, and cabbage.

FLORIDA'S SWEETEST INDUSTRY

Southern Florida is the nation's largest producer of cane sugar. The cane fields cover about 440,000 acres, an area almost the size of Lake Okeechobee. Requiring more than a year to mature, sugarcane grows over twelve feet tall. The cane is harvested from mid-October through March and is transported to one of the seven huge sugar mills in the area to be processed into sugar. The fields are first burned to remove dead leaves which would otherwise interfere with cutting and processing. In the winter months the fire and smoke from burning cane fields are common sights around the shores of Lake Okeechobee. With a payroll of $230 million, the cane industry employs nearly twenty thousand people.

Today, the cane industry is under attack from environmentalists. Much of the runoff from the cane fields is high-nutrient phosphate and other fertilizer. Although these are non-toxic pollutants, they nevertheless can cause considerable damage to the fragile ecosystem of the Everglades. Native flora that cannot tolerate high levels of nutrients are killed off and replaced by cattails and other plants that thrive on these substances.

The cane industry is also blamed by some, perhaps unjustifiably, for high levels of mercury that cause serious toxic pollution in the Everglades. The threatened Florida panther, at the top of the food chain, is in serious danger from mercury poisoning. Many streams and other bodies of water in and around the Everglades have mercury levels so high that warnings are posted not to eat fish from these waters.

Although the exact origin of the mercury is unknown, a theory proposed by some scientists is that farming of the muck lands releases minute amounts of naturally-occurring mercury which is then concentrated in the waters. Another theory is that it comes from the atmosphere where it has accumulated due to human activities. A new study by the Florida Department of Environmental Regulation indicates that garbage and medical waste incineration are the biggest sources of atmospheric mercury in Florida. Whatever the cause, dozens of lakes and many rivers have dangerous levels of mercury. Many of these are no where near the cane fields. Fortunately, Lake Okeechobee has no serious problem with mercury.

Efforts are now being made under the Everglades Forever Act to improve runoff conditions in the southern Lake Okeechobee area. Large tracts of land are being set aside to provide filtration systems to clean the water before it reaches the Everglades. But a controversial extra tax on the sugar industry to help pay the cost of the Everglades cleanup programs was defeated in the fall 1996 election.

In the southern area of Lake Okeechobee, winter vegetables are also big money crops, although they have declined in recent years in favor of cane growing.

Besides sugarcane and vegetable farming, the other large industry along the southern Lake Okeechobee shore is, of course, tourism, mainly fishing the great lake. Guide services and fishing camps/motels are plentiful in this sector. Some towns refer to themselves as the "Bass Capital of the World," but this claim can be made by many towns around the shores of Lake Okeechobee. The major communities along the southern shore are Clewiston, Lake Harbor, South Bay, and Belle Glade.

Clewiston: "America's Sweetest Town"

Clewiston had its start as a Japanese farm settlement in 1915, but it was not until the railroad was extended here from Moore Haven in 1921 that Clewiston became a real town. Named for Alonzo C. Clewis, a Tampa banker and investor, it became known as "America's Sweetest Town" when U.S. Sugar made Clewiston its corporate headquarters in 1931. During World War II, the British Royal Air Force established a training school near here. Clewiston is a sanctuary for the smooth-billed ani.

Today, outside of the tourism/fishing industry, Clewiston is still a sweet little sugar town. A good introduction to the town might start at the Clewiston Museum, downtown on Commercio Street a half block south of the main street (U.S. Route 27/State Route 98). To get to Commercio Street, proceed west on U.S. Route 27/State Route 98 just past the Clewiston Inn.

The museum, which has a full-time director, displays many artifacts from the early days of the Glades. It also contains much information about the sugar industry. Here visitors can learn about *bagasse*, the residual fiber from the sugarcane stalk when the juice has been squeezed out. After drying, it is used as fuel to generate the steam and electricity needed to operate the sugar mill. Unfortunately, for several reasons, which include the physical dangers and the threat of adverse litigation, tours of sugar mills are currently not available to the public. However, the Clewiston Museum provides a good starting place to learn more about this fascinating industry that is so important to the economy of the Glades.

Lodging

Some motels/hotels cater to the fishing crowd. For example, the Roland Martin Marina/Hotel and the Angler's Marina & Motel are both in Clewiston. For those who seek more luxurious accommodations, we recommend the Clewiston Inn.

Owned and operated by U.S. Sugar Corporation, whose headquarters are across the street, the Clewiston Inn is the center of elegant social life in Clewiston. There was a natural high sand ridge along the southern shore of Lake Okeechobee before the days of the Hoover Dike. In fact, Clewiston was known in its early days as Sand Point. The original Clewiston Inn was built in 1925-26 on this high sandy ground. Although the inn burned to the ground in 1937, a new Clewiston Inn was completed in 1938 by U.S. Sugar. It was intended to be a lodging and dining place for their executives and the public. It remains so today and is one of the finest inns in the Lake Okeechobee area. Anglers can bring their filleted catches here and the chef will prepare them with side dishes for a nominal fee. President Herbert Hoover stayed here twice, once while president-elect in 1928 and again during the dedication of the Hoover Dike in 1961. A special attraction is the wildlife mural of the Everglades in the cocktail lounge. The Clewiston Inn has been placed on the National Register of Historic Places by the Department of Interior. The food is excellent and prices are reasonable.

Dining

Besides dining at the Clewiston Inn, a visitor should try the Old Southern Bar-B-Que Pit on the main street (U.S. Route 27). Many colorful roadside signs advertise this restaurant along U.S. Route 27. It's worth a stop if only to see the huge collection of antiques.

Other Amenities

The Okeechobee Waterway passes along Clewiston's Lake Okeechobee waterfront. The Hoover Memorial Park is adjacent to the shore on the lake side of the Hoover Dike where public boat ramps allow launching directly into Lake Okeechobee. There are picnic tables and other facilities. The S-310 lock on the east side of the park allows boats to enter the lake from the rim canal.

SOUTH SIDE The Clewiston Inn, owned and operated by U.S. Sugar Corporation   Photo courtesy of South Florida Water Management District

Clewiston is a convenient base from which to visit several attractions south of the city. These include the Big Cypress Seminole Indian Reservation, The Seminole Gaming Palace, Corkscrew Swamp, and the Sunniland Oil Field Park.

The Seminoles have an active campaign to attract visitors to their reservation. Among other things, they encourage private planes to visit their airport and motorcycle groups to ride the reservation. The Seminole Visitor's Center is about thirty-five miles south of Clewiston. A new attraction is the Ah Tha Thi Ki Museum of the Seminole Tribes of Florida. Nearby is a recreational village called the Kissimmee Billy Swamp Safari, which offers overnight lodging, a cafe, airboat and swamp buggy tours, alligator and snake demonstrations, storytelling, and other activities. Jeep jamborees and additional special events are held yearly on the reservation. For more information call (800) 949-6101.

About thirty-five miles west of the Big Cypress Reservation (some fifty miles southwest of Clewiston) is the town of

SOUTH SIDE　Big Cypress Seminole Indian Reservation

SOUTH SIDE   Corkscrew Swamp boardwalk

Immokalee, where the Seminole Gaming Palace is located. Operated by the Seminole Indian Tribe, the palace offers state-of-the-art slot machines and other gambling games. There is also a small cafe inside which serves nicely prepared food.

Just a few miles west of Immokalee is the National Audubon Society's famous Corkscrew Swamp Sanctuary, which contains the world's largest bald cypress forest. A two-mile boardwalk wends its way through this idyllic natural setting. The swamp has a rich variety of native flora and fauna, including specimens of the custard apple trees that once were so numerous along the southern shore of Lake Okeechobee. Admission charges are $6.50 per adult and $3.00 for children over six years old. All visitor areas are handicap accessible. The sanctuary is open every day of the year. For more information, call (941) 657-3771.

New visitors to southern Florida are sometimes surprised to learn that the state has an active oil industry. The first oil field in Florida was discovered in 1943 by Humble Oil Corporation (now Exxon) at Sunniland, about eleven miles south of

SOUTH SIDE   Oil Field Park, Sunniland

Immokalee. The grateful state awarded Humble Oil a cash bonus of $50,000 for making the find, a lot of money in those days. Several other oil fields were found along the so-called Sunniland trend in southern Florida, the southernmost field just outside the limits of the Everglades National Park. More than 100 million barrels of oil have been found along this trend. Although the oil industry has not caused any significant environmental damage in Florida, current anti-oil industry feeling has led to a big decline in oil exploration and production has declined significantly in recent years.

Although the Sunniland Field itself has been abandoned, some oil is still being produced nearby. A small park dedicated to the discovery lies alongside State Route 29 about twelve miles south of Immokalee. An old pumping unit and an informational plaque are here as well as a picnic area.

Lake Harbor

Lake Harbor is a quiet little agricultural community on Lake Okeechobee's southern shore along the Miami Canal. Originally called Ritta, it was once the site of the famous Bolles Hotel. Promoter Richard J. Bolles built the hotel at Lake

Harbor to help sell parcels of land to would-be Glades farmers. The prospective buyers could climb to the observation tower on top of the hotel and survey their land, much of it still underwater.

Just west of the Lake Harbor is John Stretch Park on Lake Okeechobee. It has restroom facilities, covered picnic tables, a free dump station for RVs, and a pavilion that can be reserved for special gatherings. No overnight camping is permitted. Located adjacent to the Hoover Dike on the inland side, the park has a road leading over the dike to a ramp for launching boats into Lake Okeechobee. The Okeechobee Waterway lies directly in front of the launch site. The park contains many palm trees, including several clumps of paurotis palms, the so-called Everglades palm.

South Bay: "Crossroads of Florida"
South Bay originated when the North New River Canal was completed into Lake Okeechobee in 1912. Like most of the localities where canals meet Lake Okeechobee's shore, this new community was expected to become a boom town. But by 1917 there were still only a dozen or so settlers at South Bay. Today's population is 4,064 persons, most of whom have jobs or businesses related to agriculture.

Conveniently located on U.S. Route 27, the Okeechobee Inn in South Bay offers some of the better lodging in the area.

The new Southbay RV Campground just west of the town has seventy two campsites, each with water, electricity, and cable TV hookups. Rates are $75 weekly for RVs for non-residents. This neat, clean campground opened in April 1995 and has an on-site manager for security day and night. A road adjacent to the campground leads over the dike to a site where boats can be launched directly into Lake Okeechobee.

Belle Glade: "Her Soil Is Her Fortune"
Still another canal-head town, Belle Glade was founded in 1919 at the head of the Hillsboro Canal, one of the largest

canals built to take excess water from Lake Okeechobee. In spite of its relatively late start, Belle Glade is now the largest city around Lake Okeechobee, with a population of about 17,250. Principal attractions in Belle Glade include the Belle Glade Marina Campground, the Lawrence E. Will Museum, and the Dolly Hand Cultural Arts Center.

The late Lawrence E. Will was dubbed "Historian of the Glades" by the Belle Glade Chamber of Commerce. He was a man of many hats. Will was one of the earliest pioneers in the southern Lake Okeechobee area, arriving in 1913, and, through the years, he witnessed the development of this new frontier. He founded the small town of Okeelanta, about four miles south of Belle Glade, where a huge sugar mill operates today. Will was a farmer, land developer, surveyor, boatman, dredgeman, shipping agent, auto and tractor dealer, and mechanic. He also served for thirty years as the chief of Belle Glade's fire department. When the Hoover Dike was built, Will operated some of the equipment used in its construction. In his later years, Lawrence Will authored six books on the history of the Glades. Written in delightful Cracker style, these books are an invaluable source of Everglades history. The museum is adjacent to the Chamber of Commerce in downtown Belle Glade.

The Dolly Hand Cultural Arts Center is at the Palm Beach Community College in Belle Glade. Top-rated theater programs are presented here during the season, which extends from November through April.

Lodging

The Belle Glade Marina Campground on Torry Island, one of the few campgrounds directly on Lake Okeechobee, can be reached via a small wooden swing bridge that extends over the Okeechobee Waterway. The campground has 350 campsites, 2 bait and tackle shops, 8 public boat ramps, and an airboat launch site. The ramps are open to the public and are free except on weekends from 5 to 9 A.M. when a dollar per boat is charged. Prices for RVs are $14 per day or $72 per week for a full hookup. Many sites are on the water and have adjacent boat dockage. A miniature golf course is within the campground, and an eighteen-hole golf course is on the mainland, just before the campground entrance. A road formerly led from the Belle Glade Marina Campground to Kramer Island, but it is no longer in use. Kramer Island can now be reached only by boat.

Dining

A popular dining spot in Belle Glade is the Drawbridge Cafe, on the mainland just before the swing bridge to the Belle Glade Marina/Campground.

Other amenities

In late April each year, Belle Glade holds its Black Gold Festival in celebration of the year's harvest of sugarcane and other crops.

The South Bay/Belle Glade area also offers the visitor a good base from which to explore interesting places to the south and east. U.S. Route 27 continues south to pass through cane country and some of the undeveloped northern Everglades until it reaches Alligator Alley (Interstate 75), thirty-seven miles south of Okeelanta.

County Route 827 leads southeast out of Belle Glade to the Everglades Experimental Station where data regarding agriculture in the area can be obtained.

U.S. Route 441 goes east of Belle Glade about fifteen miles to Lion Country Safari and then south to the Arthur R. Marshall Loxahatchee National Wildlife Preserve.

Lion Country Safari is a privately-owned outdoor zoo where the animals are free to roam in large enclosed areas and private cars can pass through to observe the wildlife. A variety of exotic animals can be seen, including lions, elephants, and buffalo. There are also demonstrations and feedings that make the tour more enjoyable. This is probably one of the best ways to spend a day at the zoo with the youngsters. There are no time constraints on driving through the park and repeat trips can be taken the same day at no extra charge. Fees are $13.95 for adults and $9.95 for children under sixteen. Kids under three are free. Discounts are often available. Seniors and AARP members get significant reductions in fares. A kennel is available for pets, which are not allowed in cars touring the park area.

The Loxahatchee Wildlife Refuge is a huge swampland just a few miles inland from the densely populated coastal areas around West Palm Beach and Boca Raton. It is essentially a surviving part of the original Everglades. Native flora and fauna can be observed from the safety and comfort of a boardwalk. Ranger headquarters are located off U.S. Route 441, about ten miles south of Royal Palm Beach. A boardwalk through some of the swampland provides visitors a view of native flora and fauna.

13 The East Side of Lake Okeechobee

*T*he east side (as well as the west side) of Lake Okeechobee is transitional, incorporating features of both the north and south sides. It is a land of sugarcane fields, citrus groves, vegetable plots, and cattle pasturage. From Port Mayaca, the approximate midpoint on the east side, the area immediately north is largely cane fields. About five or six miles farther north, it is mostly cattle country all the way to Okeechobee. East of Port Mayaca are some huge citrus groves; to the south is cane country with a few vegetable farms.

With the opening of the West Palm Beach Canal to Canal Point in 1917 and the construction of the Connors Highway along the canal in 1923, promoters had dreams of Canal Point becoming a big city. The same was true for Port Mayaca when the St. Lucie Canal was completed from Stuart to this area in 1921. For various reasons, most towns located where canals entered Lake Okeechobee never developed into big communities. The largest town on the east coast became Pahokee. Indiantown, about ten miles east of Port Mayaca, is another large community on the east side of Lake Okeechobee. Sand Cut is a small residential community just north of Canal Point.

Pahokee

Many of the earliest communities around Lake Okeechobee originated as fishing camps. Since the rocky bottom of the lake in this area discouraged net fishing, Pahokee was late in developing. The first settlers, farmers, began moving in about 1914. The community, originally known as East Beach, then Ridgeway Beach, finally took the name Pahokee. The name comes from the Seminole word for the Everglades, Pah Hay Okee (or Pai Hai O Kee), which means "grassy waters." A Grassy Waters Festival is held in Pahokee each November.

A severe freeze in 1917 plunged the temperature in Miami to twenty-seven degrees. However, it did not freeze at Pahokee and vegetable crops survived. Consequently, the price of Pahokee's produce skyrocketed and brought wealth to many of the area's farmers. News about the productive soil and the warm climate spread quickly and a rush to the "black gold fields" was on. Pahokee prospered and became incorporated as a city in 1922. By 1930, over 2,000 people lived here while Belle Glade, the largest city around Lake Okeechobee today, counted only 950 residents.

Currently, Pahokee has 6,800 year-round residents while Belle Glade numbers more than 17,000. The majestic royal palms that line many of Pahokee's streets make a lasting

PAHOKEE MARINA & CAMPGROUND
The city-operated Pahokee Marina & Campground, one of the few campgrounds directly on the Lake Okeechobee shore, offers fifty-two full hookups for RVs and several tent sites. The park also has a fishing pier, picnic area, playground equipment, restrooms, and other amenities. Boat dockage is available at the marina and there is a bait and tackle shop. The greatest concentration of sailboats on Lake Okeechobee is centered here. There's probably no better place to view a lake sunset than the top of the Hoover Dike at Pahokee Marina & Campground. The view from here is due west into the sunset and the lake appears as an endless body of water.

EAST SIDE Pahokee Town Park with fishing pier, marina, and campground Photo courtesy of South Florida Water Management District

impression on visitors entering the town. Another attraction is Pahokee Marina and Campground, conveniently located adjacent to the downtown area.

Lodging

Unfortunately, there are no hotels or motels in Pahokee. Unless visitors have an RV or camping gear for the town park, they stay elsewhere, often at the Okeechobee Inn in South Bay, twelve miles south.

Dining

An old joke goes: "If you want a good meal in Pahokee, go home and cook it yourself." It's true that there aren't many restaurants in town, but that joke is not fair any more. Pam's Seafood Restaurant & Market on U.S. Route 441/State Route 98, just a couple of blocks south of the Chamber of Commerce in downtown Pahokee, serves excellent food. Their fresh Okeechobee catfish meals are outstanding. There are also three fast-food franchises near the downtown area. The Elks Club, on the main street just north of the Chamber of

Commerce, has started offering a lunch from eleven to two that is open to the public. For something a little unusual, try the new Captain's Galley, a floating restaurant tied up at the Pahokee Town Park Marina. The same owners offer sight-seeing and dinner tours on a larger boat moored at the marina. Captain JP Boat Cruises has cruises across the lake, around the lake, and through the locks on the Okeechobee Waterway. In the summer, this company takes its big boat to the New York area for cruises. For Okeechobee trips, call (407) 924 2100.

Other points of interest in Pahokee include the Historic Museum and Pioneer Park.

The museum is downtown in the same building as the Pahokee Chamber of Commerce. It contains artifacts and mementos of the early days in the Pahokee area. Pioneer Park is on Becom Avenue (State Route 715) just a couple of miles from downtown on the east side of the road. It is actually a cemetery where many of the victims of the 1928 hurricane are buried. A small plaque honors their memory.

After some years of stagnation, Pahokee seems to be back on track to becoming a growing town again. The Chamber of Commerce reports that fifteen new businesses were started in 1995. The new Esmore Youth Offenders Facility opened here in 1996, creating two hundred new jobs. It would appear that a hotel or motel would be a good investment and the town could use some more good restaurants. Perhaps one day, residents and visitors will congregate daily at the top of the Hoover Dike in Pahokee Marina and Campground to have a festive time and enjoy the beautiful sunsets as they do at Mallory Square in Key West.

Port Mayaca

Port Mayaca is directly on the Okeechobee Waterway, at the confluence of the St. Lucie Canal and Lake Okeechobee. There are some nice old homes along the highway in Port Mayaca. However, it remains only a very small community which

EAST SIDE   Weekend fishing for specks at Port Myaca

never achieved the size promoters hoped for when the St. Lucie Canal opened. Two points of interest are the Port Mayaca Lock and the Port Mayaca Cemetery.

The Port Mayaca Lock is directly on the Cross Florida Waterway (Okeechobee Waterway) and is the busiest lock on the lake. Visitors can pull into a large parking area on either side of the canal and watch the lock operations. The top of the Hoover Dike offers a splendid view of Lake Okeechobee and it is another great place to view a sunset. This area is a popular recreational fishing spot, especially on weekends. Cormorants are usually abundant here. There are no restroom facilities or refreshment stands.

State Route 76, which runs along the south side of the St. Lucie Canal, leads east three and a half miles to the Port Mayaca Cemetery, where there is a mass burial site for victims of the 1928 hurricane. A memorial plaque inscription indicates that 1,600 unidentified bodies are buried in the common grave.

Indiantown

The second largest community in the east side area of Lake Okeechobee is Indiantown, near the St. Lucie Canal about twelve miles east of Port Mayaca. Native Americans, both the original natives of the Lake Okeechobee area and the Seminoles, lived on the high ground of Indiantown and the area around it. The sandy soil here is more suited to citrus groves than to cane. Along State Route 76 toward Indiantown, the cane fields of Port Mayaca quickly give way to large orange groves.

About twelve miles south of Indiantown is another naturally high area. Unreachable today except on foot, it is the location of the so-called Big Mound, or Big Mound City. After the Battle of Okeechobee was fought on Christmas Day, 1837, a band of Indians fled to these mounds. Some of the Indians were later captured here by federal soldiers who were amazed at the elaborate arrangement of the mounds. Only preliminary archaeological work has been done at this site and nothing spectacular has been reported so far. However, these mounds apparently pre-date the arrival of Europeans in Florida.

Some special attractions near Indiantown include the Seminole Inn, Owens Grove, Payson Park, Barley Barber Swamp, Indiantown Marina, the Dupuis Wildlife and Environmental Area, and the J. W. Corbett Wildlife Management Area.

The Seminole Inn, in the center of Indiantown, provides some of the finest lodging and dining in the Lake Okeechobee area. The inn, which features massive stone walls, cypress ceilings, and hardwood floors, was built in the 1920s by S. Davies Warfield, a Baltimore banker who planned to make Indiantown the headquarters for his Seaboard Railroad. His niece, Wallis Warfield, served as hostess at the Seminole Inn in the early days. Wallis went on to become the Duchess of Windsor when she married the King of England, who abdicated his throne for her. The 1920s ambiance of the Seminole Inn is graced with all the modern conveniences. Phone (407) 597-3777.

Owens Grove, near downtown Indiantown, is a privately

owned enterprise consisting of a commercial citrus grove, a small packing facility, and a restored Cracker house dating from 1911. Some of the floors and walls of the restored house were built with Dade County heart pine, a favorite building material of the early days. Many relics and antiques are displayed in the tin-roofed structure. Although the shop and house are the main attractions, the nature trail offers a delightful short walk through a beautiful hardwood hammock. Huge laurel oak trees are draped with vines, creating a Garden-of-Eden effect. Exotic peacocks stroll the grounds. This idyllic setting is definitely worth a visit.

Owens Grove is just seven-tenths of a mile from the center of Indiantown. To reach it from the main street (State Route 710/Warfield Boulevard), turn west on Adams Avenue (at the traffic light), proceed past the post office, and take a dogleg left-right across the railroad tracks. Owens Grove is on the left about a half-mile down SW Farm Road. The grove is open Monday through Friday, 8:30 A.M. to 5:30 P.M., and Saturdays from 8:30 A.M. until 2 P.M. (closed Sundays). There is no admission charge.

EAST SIDE Restored Cracker house, Owens Grove, Indiantown

EAST SIDE   Heading for the morning workout at Payson Park
Thoroughbred Training Grounds near Indiantown
Photo courtesy of South Florida Water Management District

Payson Park, east of Indiantown on State Route 76, is one of the largest thoroughbred training tracks in the country. Horses are trained here for the Hialeah, Gulfstream, and Calder race courses from October to May. Visitors can enjoy breakfast or lunch at the small cafe in the park and watch the morning workouts. There is no admission charge.

Florida Power's huge Martin County electrical generating plant, a few miles northwest of Indiantown on State Route 710, is the site of the Barley Barber Swamp. Replete with native wildlife and plants, this 420-acre nature preserve on Florida Power's property features a mile-long boardwalk. Bald eagles nest here. Admission and guided tours are free, but trips must be prearranged. Call (800) 257-9267 for reservations.

The Indiantown Marina lies along the St. Lucie Canal where boats can be moored in the fresh water of the canal yet be a short distance from the salt water of the Atlantic. It has thirty-four slips and offers transient and more permanent accommodations for vessels up to 145 feet long. Boats of various sizes from all over the world are found here. There are also a few RV hookups and campsites. To reach the marina,

EAST SIDE Boardwalk in the Barley Barber Swamp near Indiantown Photo courtesy of South Florida Water Management District

EASTT SIDE Indiantown Marina on the St. Lucie Canal Photo courtesy of South Florida Water Management District

take the same dogleg across the railroad tracks as to Owens Grove (see above), but then turn left onto Fennel Road. The marina is about eight-tenths of a mile from the downtown area.

The Dupuis Wildlife and Environmental Area is a 21,875-acre wilderness area available for hiking, bicycling, camping, hunting in season, and horseback riding. The site is accessible from State Route 76 between Port Mayaca and Indiantown. Gate 3 is the equestrian sector where stalls are available for $3 per day, and over thirty miles of trails are open for riders. The area at gate 2 has thirty-five miles of hiking trails. There is a $1 per day charge for parking. The Florida Division of Forestry manages the Dupuis reserve. For further information call (407) 924-5310.

Located about ten miles southeast of Indiantown on State Route 710, the 60,224-acre J. W. Corbett Wildlife Management Area is a scrub and swampland area set aside primarily for hunting and fishing. Backpack camping is encouraged during the recreational season (from the last weekend in April through the Sunday two weeks before the opening of archery season in August). During the archery and gun seasons, camping is permitted only at designated sites. A nature boardwalk enables visitors to enjoy native flora and fauna. The area is managed by the Florida Game and Fresh Water Fish commission. For further information call (407) 640-6100.

Canal Point

This small community, first settled about 1909, was called various names including New Town, Long Beach, and Nemaha until the West Palm Beach Canal here was finished in 1917. From then on it was called Canal Point. The canal was an important water transportation link to Lake Okeechobee for West Palm Beach and other communities in eastern Palm Beach County. The Connors Highway was completed along the side of the canal in 1929 and, from this point, the road continued northeast to Okeechobee. The Canal Point Park and Jones Fish House are two of the town's highlights.

Canal Point Park is adjacent to the junction of the West Palm Beach Canal and Lake Okeechobee, on the lake side of the Hoover Dike. It offers boat ramps, picnic areas, a good scenic view, and a fine place to watch the sunset. There is a plaque honoring William J. "Fingy" Connors, the man who built the highway from West Palm Beach to Okeechobee which passes through Canal Point. The highway bridge over the canal and the banks of the canal are popular fishing spots.

Just past the park, on U.S. Route 441, is Jones Fish House, one of the few remaining commercial fisheries on Lake Okeechobee. The industry, particularly catfishing, boomed in the years between the early 1900s and the 1940s. Fresh fish, mostly catfish, are brought in daily to Jones Fish House to be cleaned and processed for shipment to other parts of the country. A visitor can buy a pound or more of fresh fish here and watch the operations of a commercial fish house.

14 The Wild West Side
of Lake Okeechobee

*T*he west side of Lake Okeechobee might be called the *wild* west side. Cowboys, Indians, hunters, fishers, frog giggers, and party lovers live and visit here. It is the most remote and undeveloped area around the lake. Like the east coast, it is a transitional zone between the northern sector, largely cattle country, and the southern area, mostly sugar-cane farms. This is "gloriously natural" Glades County, a huge geographical area about the size of Lake Okeechobee itself. It borders the western forty-five miles of the Lake Okeechobee shoreline.

Much of the county (over 60 percent) is cattle and other agriculture lands owned or leased by the Lykes Brothers conglomerate. Howell Tyson Lykes, a medical doctor, purchased large tracts of Florida land in the mid-1800s. He soon quit the medical field to pursue business interests which included shipping cattle to Cuba. His seven sons carried on the family business and, today, their descendants run huge Lykes Bros., Inc., headquartered in Tampa. Lykes is one of Florida's largest landowners, with extensive cattle ranches and citrus groves. The company is also involved in shipping, insurance, residential development, and other businesses.

In all of Glades County there are only eight thousand residents. The biggest town and county seat, Moore Haven, has just fifteen hundred residents. Other communities on the west side of Lake Okeechobee, all in Glades County, include Buckhead Ridge (about eight miles south of Okeechobee), Lakeport (on Fisheating Creek, about midway down the west side), and, farther west away from the lake, Ortona and Palmdale. The communities adjacent to the lake are fishing and tourism centers as well as agricultural towns.

Moore Haven

Moore Haven originated with James A. Moore, a developer and promoter who laid out the town in 1915. Moore induced people like Alton B. Parker, Teddy Roosevelt's presidential opponent, to invest in land nearby. He also persuaded William Jennings Bryan, the famous orator, to help promote the town.

In less than two years, Moore was forced to sell. New investors included Marian O'Brien, a wealthy woman from Philadelphia who became mayor of Moore Haven — the first elected woman mayor in the United States. Marian, dubbed the "Duchess of Moore Haven," helped promote the town and it was soon a thriving agricultural center. The first sugar mill in the Everglades was established in Moore Haven, although it did not operate for long.

O'Brien and her husband, backed by Alonzo C. Clewis, a Tampa banker, laid out the new town of Clewiston and built the first railroad over the muck lands from Moore Haven to Clewiston in 1921.

A series of natural disasters befell Moore Haven, including severe flooding of the farmlands in 1922 and the hurricane of 1926, which nearly wiped out the town. During this awesome storm, more than 150 town residents lost their lives.

Today, Moore Haven is a quiet little fishing, tourist, and agricultural center of 1,500 year-round residents on busy U.S. Route 27. It is the county seat of Glades County. At Moore Haven, the Caloosahatchee River is connected to Lake Okeechobee via the Moore Haven Lock. The Alvin L. Ward Sr. Memorial Park is on the east side of the river.

WEST SIDE   Dockage on the Caloosahatchee River at Moore Haven

The Caloosahatchee River flows through the center of Moore Haven, providing the western link for the Cross Florida/Okeechobee Waterway. Historically, the river did not connect to the lake, but it was dredged and connected by Hamilton Disston's crews in the late 1800s.

The Moore Haven Lock is directly on the Okeechobee Waterway and, after Port Mayaca, is the second busiest lock on the lake, with nearly 20,000 vessels locking through each year. The lock is operated by the U.S. Army Corps of Engineers. The area adjacent to the lock provides a scenic view of the Hoover Dike and Lake Okeechobee. Everything from large ocean-going tugs, barges, and yachts to tiny canoes and rowboats pass through this lock, and all get the same courteous treatment as they are locked through at no charge, either into Lake Okeechobee from the Caloosahatchee River or the reverse. Below the lock, on the river, is a popular fishing spot where large snook are often caught.

The Alvin L. Ward Sr. Memorial Park, on the lake side of the Hoover Dike, has five ramps for launching boats directly into Lake Okeechobee. Although overnight camping is not allowed, there are picnic areas, a playground, and restrooms.

Lodging

The Rice Hotel is on the main street. The Glades Inn, a mile south on U.S. Route 27, underwent renovation in 1996. For RV operators and tenters, the Moore Haven Yacht Club and Sportsman's Marina have facilities. The Yacht Club is on the inland side of the Hoover Dike, adjacent to the lock, while the Sportsman's Marina is on the Lake Okeechobee side of the dike. The Yacht Club often gives RVers a night or two free if they are willing to listen to an hour's sales promotion.

Dining

The Moore Haven Restaurant, the Glades Inn Restaurant, Dairy King (Chinese food), and a Subway sandwich shop are along the main street. The surprising absence of fast-food franchises along this busy highway through town is due to the lack of a town sewer system. Reportedly, a Burger King franchise will open soon despite this.

Other Amenities

Lundy's Hardware Store is a block south of the main street. With its old-fashioned decor, this store is a favorite of those interested in old buildings and local color.

Moore Haven has an annual Chalo Nitka Festival in March to celebrate the arrival of spring. The festival, held each year for the past fifty years, features a parade, livestock show, rodeo, carnival rides, dances, and other activities. Chalo Nitka means big bass in the Seminole language. Seminoles are active participants in the big festival.

Ortona

Ortona is on the west bank of the Caloosahatchee River about eleven miles due west of Moore Haven on State Route 78. Attractions here include the Ortona Lock and the Ortona Indian Mounds. The Ortona Lock is busy with the constant Cross-Florida/Okeechobee Waterway boat traffic. From either side of the river there is a good view of the operation.

Adjacent to the lock on the west bank is a small park with picnic facilities and a ramp for launching boats into the river. A $2 fee is charged for the use of the ramp.

The Indian mounds just east of Ortona are the only ones in the Lake Okeechobee area that can be easily visited (See Chapter 2). Next to the mounds is the Ortona Cemetery, the resting place of many of the 1926 hurricane victims killed in Moore Haven. Seminole chief Billy Bowlegs III, who died in 1965 at the age of 103, is also buried here.

Palmdale

Palmdale is a small community along the banks of Fisheating Creek about eighteen miles northwest of Moore Haven on U.S. Route 27. Two interesting attractions in Palmdale are Gatorama and Cypress Kneeland.

Gatorama is a privately owned alligator farm which sells alligator hides and meat to customers. Although there is an admission fee, it is well worth the money to see some of the scaly-backed behemoths at the farm. It has some unbelievably

WEST SIDE   Tom Gaskin's Cypress Kneeland Museum at Palmdale   Photo courtesy of South Florida Water Management District

huge alligators and crocodiles as well as several mutant alligators. Recently, Gatorama, now in operation for over forty years, was designated a National Historical Landmark.

Cypress Kneeland began when the legendary Tom Gaskins (now retired) moved his cypress knee factory from Arcadia to Palmdale in 1937. He manufactured various pieces of furniture and other articles from the knobby knees of cypress trees. A fiercely independent local character, Tom had many unique signs advertising his shop and museum along U.S. Route 27. The museum and shop are now run by his son, Tom Jr. Admission is by voluntary donation.

Lakeport

Although isolated and remote, Lakeport is well-known to many world-traveling sports enthusiasts, writers, celebrities, and others as a first-class destination for hunters and fishers. Several TV documentaries have been filmed here to show the remarkable abundance of wildlife. Only one thousand residents live here year round.

Located near the middle of the west side of Lake Okeechobee, Lakeport is along that wide, marshy area of the lake which teems with life. Here are the greatest numbers of alligators, frogs, snakes, and birds in this natural wonderland. This area provides some of the finest duck hunting in Florida. Wild turkey, hog, and deer are also hunted in this area.

Rumored to be a bit of a party town, Lakeport boasts many fine homes both along the rim canal and inland. Many Floridians from the seacoast towns of Sarasota, Tampa, Miami, and others own weekend and vacation homes here. It is a great place to get away from the crowds and enjoy nature at its finest.

The town stretches for about six miles along State Route 78, which runs adjacent and parallel to the west shore of Lake Okeechobee. The southern end of Lakeport begins near the point where Fisheating Creek enters Lake Okeechobee. The Harney Pond Canal enters the lake about four miles up the highway. Margaret Van de Velde Park is located where Harney Pond Canal meets the lake.

Fisheating Creek is one of the three principal natural streams flowing into Lake Okeechobee (the others are the Kissimmee River and Taylor Creek). It is the single one that remains essentially in its natural condition. Its headwaters are some fifty miles north near Sebring. Just before entering Lakeport from the south on State Route 78, there is a small park with a ramp for launching boats into Fisheating Creek. This stream then leads a short distance into Lake Okeechobee. This area and the three miles of State Route 78 south of this point are inside the Hoover Dike. The dike extends west away from Lake Okeechobee along both the north and south sides of the Fisheating Creek floodplain. This is the only place around the entire lake where the highway passes any appreciable distance inside the dike.

The Harney Pond Canal is one of the largest canals connected to Lake Okeechobee. It drains a large area of cattle range west of the lake. Where the canal enters the lake there is a break in the Hoover Dike, but the canal is leveed on both sides for several miles away from the lake. Adjacent to the south side of the canal, where Route 78 crosses, is Margaret Van de Velde Park. This site has a large parking lot, three boat ramps, small fishing piers, a picnic area, restrooms, and a boardwalk that leads to an observation platform. It is a great spot for observing the bird life in the marshy west side of Lake Okeechobee.

Just north of the Harney Pond Canal is the junction of State Route 78 with County Road 721. Glenn Hunter's RV Park-Store and Guide Service, Lakeport Lodge and Restaurant, and the Duck Pub are found at this intersection. Glenn Hunter is one of the best-known guides on Lake Okeechobee, having been featured on numerous television shows and in many national magazines.

Another well-known dining spot in Lakeport is the Calusa Lodge, just south of the Harney Pond Canal. The collection of bass trophies on the walls is definitely worth a stop.

Lakeport holds an annual Sour Orange Festival in February. The sour orange trees in the vicinity are root stocks from orange trees that were killed by freezes.

About five miles north of Lakeport, where the highway crosses the Indian Prairie Canal, is the Indian Prairie Campground. The campground, along the south bank of the canal, is a primitive RV/tent campsite operated by the U.S. Army Corps of Engineers. There is no charge for staying at this camp. A large group campground is also here. A permit is required for group camping and there is a $25 charge per group. Phone: (941) 983-8101.

Buckhead Ridge

Buckhead Ridge is a small community of houses, mobile homes, and RV parks on the west shore of Lake Okeechobee. It is near the south bank of the Kissimmee River at the northern extremity of Glades County. Many of the homes are on the rim canal or on waterways that link to the rim canal. Near the center of the community, boats can access Lake

WEST SIDE   Brighton Seminole Indian Reservation, a cattle and agricultural area   Photo courtesy of South Florida Water Management District

Okeechobee through a small lock. Catering to the early fishing crowd, the Buckhead Ridge Marina and Restaurant is open from 6 A.M. to 2 P.M.

Southwest of Buckhead Ridge and a short distance west of Lakeport is the Brighton Seminole Indian Reservation. This 35,000-acre reservation is home to about four hundred Seminole Indians, most engaged in cattle ranching and agriculture. There are craft shops open to the public and an RV resort park on the reservation. The major annual event is the Brighton Field Day and Rodeo in February. A new bingo and gaming hall, open Monday through Saturday, is attracting large crowds. Bingo games begin each day at 6:45 P.M. Bicycle and hiking tours through the reservation can be arranged. For further information, the tribal field office can be reached at (941) 763-4128.

Part 3 THE FUTURE

15 Change Is on the Way

*T*hings are changing in Okeechobeeland, with increasing emphasis placed on environmental and ecological factors.

In the immediate future, the sugarcane industry, long blamed for much of the Everglade's pollution, will continue to be an important part of the economy, providing critical jobs for a large number of people. As a result of increased environmental awareness, however, the industry is taking steps to reduce its pollution of the Everglades. And additional cane fields will be purchased by the government to be set aside as filtering marshes.

A factor affecting the long-term future of sugarcane is the soil. The rich muck lands are a finite asset. Over the years, the nutrients necessary to grow cane are exhausted. The soil becomes poorer and is no longer able to support good growths. The depleted soil, however, can be used for citrus trees. Many former cane fields have been converted to citrus, and there are now thousands of acres of young groves in the Glades. Previously, citrus had not been a major cash crop in most of the area immediately around Lake Okeechobee. The ideal subtropical climate with its rare freezes is leading to an increased number of orange, grapefruit, and lime groves.

Another factor effecting the future of sugarcane may come from overseas. Many of the local folks believe that if Cuba rejoins the Free World, there will be a considerable impact on the industry. Cheaper Cuban sugar may be imported, which could reduce the demand for the U.S.-grown product. And, if workers return to Cuba, there is the potential for losing their cane-growing expertise. Many of Florida's cane workers are Cuban, including several top executives.

The dairy industry, long blamed for much of the pollution of Lake Okeechobee, is now strictly controlling runoff. Okeechobee County will continue to be Florida's biggest dairy land and beef cattle will remain an important industry.

The new growth industry, however, is ecotourism. Improvements in the Florida National Scenic Trail will have a big effect on the tourist business in Okeechobeeland. The Master Plan, created by Florida's Department of Transportation, anticipates high-intensity usage of the trail on top of the Hoover Dike. Plans include the construction of trailheads and bypasses for the locks, rivers, and other impediments along the trail. Shelters and restrooms will be built. Eventually, there will be a wheelchair-accessible paved road on top of the dike. Hikers, bikers, skaters, and others will be attracted to this new pathway. An equestrian trail at a lower level on the dike is being discussed. These trail improvement projects will cost millions of dollars and require several years to complete. However, when finished, there is little doubt that additional thousands of visitors will be drawn by the natural beauty of the area and the opportunity to view it from atop this panoramic vantage point. Herbert Hiller, a Florida writer and promoter of Florida's natural world, declares, "There will be 50,000 persons a year using the top of the Hoover Dike." Hiller could be wrong. There may be far fewer people using the trail. On the other hand, there may be far more. Only time will tell.

There will continue to be organized annual hiking and biking events for group tours around the lake. Some believe the future will bring an interest in yearly foot and bicycle races, with cash prizes for the winners. "Big O" races may become a top sporting event.

To support this increased activity, more service facilities will be required. Planners foresee a string of bed and breakfast inns along the route around the lake. Ideally, Pahokee should have at least one lodging place other than the campsites in its town park. Bike shops, horse stables, and more fishing, hunting, and nature guides will be needed.

Despite the cattle, cane, citrus, and other industries around Lake Okeechobee, the area has had a relatively high unemployment rate for the past several years. Most of the planners and thinkers around Lake Okeechobee believe many new jobs will come from ecotourism. This is the new buzz word for tours offered to visitors who want to see less of theme parks and more of real Florida.

The flora and fauna are generally recognized as two of the greatest natural resources of Okeechobeeland which draw visitors to the area. After so many years of exploitation, abuse, and neglect, the natural world around and in the lake is making a remarkable comeback. And the Lake Okeechobee area is an important part of the Florida Greenway system.

The Greenway concept is a national program to create corridors of publicly or privately owned spaces that are protected for recreational or conservation purposes. In many places, they will serve as safe migration paths for wildlife. The Florida Greenways Project was created by the state in 1991 with the intent of connecting parks and environmental hubs across the state in so-called "green belts." The common characteristic of Greenways, according to Florida's Water Management Districts, is that they go somewhere. Connected by the Florida National Scenic Trail, the Okeechobee segment leads south to the Big Cypress Swamp and the Everglades. To the north it connects with the trail which leads eventually to the Panhandle.

Bird life, so important to ecotourism, should continue to increase in Okeechobeeland. Restoration of the Kissimmee River floodplain wetlands will have a positive impact on bird life. Other projects, such as the planting of native trees,

NORTH SIDE Okeechobeeland's natural resources are its future
Photo courtesy of South Florida Water Management District

should help improve the bird population.

Some environmentalists are appalled at the U.S. Army Corps of Engineer's insistence that the sides of the Hoover Dike be mowed with the precision of a suburban lawn. Some nature lovers would like to see trees planted on the thousands of acres along the sides of the dike. Cypress and custard apple, they say, should be reintroduced at the water's edge to provide a haven for more wildlife.

Forest Michael of Michael and Michael, the planning engineering firm for the Florida National Scenic Trail, believes it will be hard to sell the Army on planting trees along the dike. He says, "The U.S. Army Corps of Engineers repeatedly states that its main function and concern around Lake Okeechobee is the protection of citizens and their property. The Corps says ity needs to keep the dike clear so that it can be inspected for leaks that might endanger the area."

The dike does leak during times of high water. In 1995, during a period of particularly high water, the dike oozed in several places along the southern and eastern shores. But there are local spots along the northern and western shores, such as the floodplain of Fisheating Creek, where the planting of native trees, like cypress, hackberry, and custard apple, presumably would not compromise safety.

Vickie Silver, senior planner for Palm Beach County, sees another problem with reforestation along the dike. "There are no cypress or custard apple nurseries where we could get the young trees," she says. Perhaps such a nursery might be a good business venture.

Certain environmentalists dream of a day when the Hoover Dike is torn down and the area returned to its original condition. They think a dike should not have been constructed in the first place, that settlers ought to have followed the wisdom of the natives, living on high ground instead of building on lowlands and depending on dikes to protect them and their property.

Some people say its wrong to interfere with nature — that it is asking for trouble. Maybe so, and perhaps the dike should never have been built, but it was. Most engineers and town planners believe the dike is here to stay. They say that there is simply no practical way the entire area could be restored in the foreseeable future. Given that the dike will remain, the majority of the environmentalists and others are now working together to make the most of it. They believe that using the dike for ecotourism is a great idea whose time has come.

Part of the overall cleanup and restoration of the ecosystem will be the ongoing attempts to eradicate exotics, especially melaleuca trees, and to replace them with native plants. The battle against water exotics like hyacinth and hydrilla will continue.

All of this environmental work has created and will continue to create jobs. Additional jobs would become available if light industries moved into the area. These industries might be attracted by the environment, living conditions, excellent schools, and sizable labor pool.

Crime is a big problem in Florida, which is unfortunate for the state but, ironically, beneficial for Okeechobeeland. As a result of Florida's recent crackdown, a new and big employer

EAST SIDE   Sunset over Lake Okeechobee from area just
south of Pahokee

around the lake is the Department of Corrections. "Ten years ago," says Harry Singletary Jr., Secretary, Florida Department of Corrections, "there were 38,000 prison beds in the state. Today there are 64,000."

In 1991, the average inmate served about 22 percent of his or her sentence. Currently, the government is committed to ending early releases. That, of course, increases the need for prison facilities. Four institutions have been constructed at a cost of over twenty million dollars each in the Okeechobee area — at Okeechobee, Pahokee, Belle Glade, and Moore Haven.

These prisons provide a work force that is at the disposal of county officials. Singletary says inmates will be available for any project for which the county needs help. "Whatever it takes to help the community, we want to do," he said at the dedication of the latest new prison, the Okeechobee Correctional Institution, in January 1996. That prison was built at a cost of thirty million dollars and will provide seven hundred jobs with an annual payroll of about twenty million dollars.

Already a large number of inmates are in evidence on state and county road work projects. The additional work force may be a great opportunity to help maintain in pristine condition the various parks around Lake Okeechobee. The condition of public facilities is always an important factor in attracting and impressing visitors.

One of these days Moore Haven will have a sewer system and the town will then have more restaurants, hotels, and other businesses. Furthermore, according to the Moore Haven Chamber of Commerce, there is a plan underway to reroute and improve U.S. Route 27 through Moore Haven. The old drawbridge across the Caloosahatchee River will be replaced.

Leland Dyalls, a native Floridian, surveyor, and thirty-year resident of Okeechobee, says, "What this area needs most is some good roads." The big cane, citrus, and cattle trucks must use a generally poor road system. The only really decent road is U.S. 27, but it is limited to the southern area. Dyalls thinks a better road system would also attract more industry.

In spite of problems such as poor roads, pollution, and high unemployment facing Okeechobeeland, one can sense that this is an area on the move. Changes are coming, and many of them will be for the better.

Sunset viewing from the top of the dike will be increasingly enjoyed by visitors and residents. Perhaps a Mallory Square (Key West) type of festivity will be promoted in some spots. At Mallory Square, residents and tourists turn out nightly for the sunset. It is a gala affair with entertainment such as mimes, animal acts, and jugglers, and food is sold from portable carts. Pahokee Marina and Compound is an ideal setting for this type of event. The view from the dike here at sunset is stunning — due west, over the seemingly endless, shimmering lake.

APPENDIX 1

Driving Tour Around Lake Okeechobee (Clockwise)

*T*his tour follows main highways and, alternatively, some side roads that pass closest to Lake Okeechobee. Surprisingly, it's possible to drive almost entirely around the "Big O" (Lake Okeechobee) on roads a couple of hundred or so yards from the lake and not see its water because of the Herbert Hoover Dike. This massive earthen work, built for hurricane protection, averages thirty-four feet in elevation above sea level and extends for nearly 110 miles around the lakeshore. Only at the Kissimmee River, Fisheating Creek, and two canal inlets on the west side are there breaks in the dike. At these four places, subsidiary dikes connected to the Hoover Dike extend away from Lake Okeechobee for a considerable distance along the banks of the streams. Also, between the highway and the Hoover Dike, along much of the shore of the lake, there is a water-filled rim canal adjacent to the big levee.

Despite the impediments to viewing Lake Okeechobee, there are more than twenty-six sites where the lake can be reached by car, bicycle, or on foot. These access points can be used for fishing, picnics, scenic views, a rendezvous with a bicycling or hiking group and, at most of them, to put a boat either directly into Lake Okeechobee or into the rim canal. If a boat is launched on the rim canal, a lock must be passed through to enter Lake Okeechobee. At some of the rim canal launch sites, the nearest lock may be several miles away.

Besides the "Big O" and the flora and fauna, there are

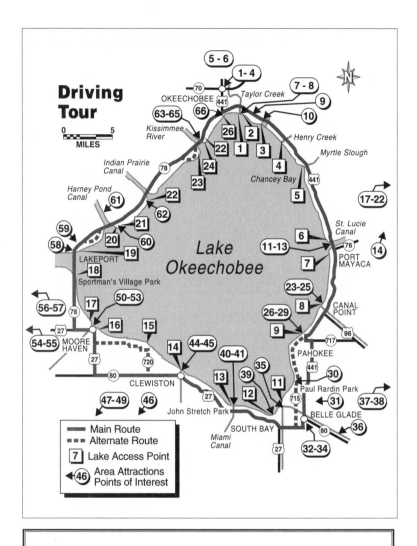

Driving Tour

0   5
MILES

LAKE ACCESS POINTS

1. West side of Taylor Creek
2. East side of Taylor Creek
3. Nubbin Slough
4. Henry Creek
5. Chancey Bay
6. North side of St. Lucie Canal at Port Myaca
7. South side of St. Lucie Canal at Port Myaca
8. Canal Point Town Park
9. Pahokee Marina and Campground
10. Paul Rardin Park
11. Belle Glade Marina Campground
12. South Bay Campground
13. John Stretch Park

14. Hoover Memorial Park, Clewiston
15. Uncle Joe's Fish Camp
16. Alvin L. Ward Sr. Park, east side of the Caloosahatchee River
17. Moore Haven Lock
18. Sportsman's Village
19. Fisheating Creek Park
20. Margaret Van de Velde Park
21. Bare Beach
22. Indian Prairie Canal
23. Northwest side of Kissimmee River
24. Okee-Tantie Recreation Area
25. C. Scott Driver Jr. Recreation Area
26. Jaycee Park (Lock 7)

AREA ATTRACTIONS/POINTS OF INTEREST

1. Okeechobee
2. Okeechobee Livestock Market
3. Okeechobee Historical Museum
4. Freedman Raulerson House
5. Larsen Dairy Farm
6. Cooper's Dark Hammock Ranch
7. Taylor Creek
8. Taylor Creek Lock
9. Battle of Okeechobee Monument
10. Nubbin Slough
11. Port Mayaca

many other attractions in the area. These include two Seminole Indian reservations, museums, ancient native mounds, historic sites, marinas, and several parks — some with boardwalks wending through natural wonderlands.

For convenience, the log is broken down into three legs. Leg 1 extends from Okeechobee to Pahokee, Leg 2 from Pahokee to Moore Haven, and Leg 3 from Moore Haven back to Okeechobee. Mileage was measured by automobile odometer.

Leg 1: Near Okeechobee to downtown Pahokee: 34.9 miles

00.0   Starting point: The intersection (traffic light) of U.S. Route 441/State Route 98 and State Route 78, three miles south of the center of the city of Okeechobee, and the south end of Parrott Avenue, adjacent to the rim canal and the Hoover Dike.

This was the approximate site where Fingey Connors, the man who brought the Tin Lizzie to Okeechobee, built his mansion on the Lake Okeechobee waterfront in the 1920s.

From this point, it is thirty-one miles to Canal Point and seventy-five miles to West Palm Beach.

Proceed east on U.S. Route 441/State Route 98, the Connors Highway.

Trees along the road include live oak, cypress, and sabal palm. The sabal, or cabbage palm is the state tree. Spanish moss and bromeliads hang from utility wires. Numerous mobile home parks, RV resorts, and fishing camps are located along the road for several miles east.

00.1   Euler's Cycling & Fitness Shop is on the right. This is one of the few bike shops in the area, offering new bicycles, equipment, and rentals for riding the Hoover Dike or taking other tours.

00.9   Big Lake Marina is on the right.

Large pastures for beef cattle and hayfields can be seen to the north.

01.1   Stardust Lanes Bowling Alley is on the left.

01.6   Pier II/Days Inn Motel and Lounge is on the right. It is one of the better accommodations in the greater Okeechobee area. Like many of the commercial places along the rim canal, this motel has its own ramp for launching boats into the canal. Boaters then can travel about a half mile east to the Taylor Creek Lock for access into Lake Okeechobee. Use of the boat ramp is, of course, permitted only to hotel guests.

Lakeside Restaurant is on the left. It is the home of the world-famous Okeeburger.

01.8   Brahma Bull Restaurant and Lounge, on the left, is one of the finest restaurants in the greater Okeechobee area. Don't miss the pictures on the wall, especially the one of the huge alligator from Lake Okeechobee. This behemoth was reportedly sixteen feet long and weighed seventeen hundred pounds!

01.9   Taylor Creek Lodge is on the right. It is a mobile home and RV park with a marina.

Lake Access: The road adjacent to the Taylor Creek Lodge (SE 27th Ct) is a service road that leads to the S-135 pump station and an office of the Florida Fresh Water Fish and Game Commission. Although the commission has a boat ramp that leads into the rim canal, this launch site is not available to the public. However, one can park here and walk or bike over the canal bridge to the top of the Hoover Dike. The commission offers free brochures and other information to the public. From the top of the dike, look for the small stand of hackberry trees on the lake side of the canal, just west of the lock. This is a favorite roosting site for turkey vultures and black vultures. Also, a couple of species of wading birds come here in the evening to roost in the hackberries. Fishing around the Taylor Creek Lock is not permitted.

02.0   Taylor Creek Bridge. This is a drawbridge that allows passage for sailboats on Taylor Creek. The Taylor Creek lock that provides boaters access to Lake Okeechobee can be seen to the right.

Lake Access: Just across the bridge, to the right, is an access service road for the lock with a public boat ramp that leads into the rim canal. One can drive, bike, or hike to the top of the Hoover Dike from this road.

Zachary Taylor Camping Resort, on the left, is one of the best RV parks in the area. It has a lovely setting on the east bank of Taylor Creek and many of the campsites have private docking. The campground also has a ramp for launching boats into Taylor Creek. Boaters can then head the short distance down the creek to the lock for access into Lake Okeechobee.

TAYLOR CREEK

Taylor Creek, one of the three principal natural inlets into Lake Okeechobee, runs through downtown Okeechobee. The town's first settlements were along the banks of the creek. The natural flow of Taylor Creek water is now controlled by the lock and a pump station just west of the lock.

02.3   The Wanta Linga Hotel/Motel is on the left. It has good overnight accommodations.

Nix's Fishing Headquarters is on the left. This is worth a stop if only to view the huge rattlesnake mounted on the front wall. This awesome creature was taken in the farmlands about twenty miles north of Okeechobee.

02.4   Brewski's Lounge and Restaurant is on the left. It has a large lounge and a small dining area where good food is served.

The Treasure Island watertower is on the left.

02.6   VFW Big Lake Post 10539 is on the right. They have bingo on Thursdays at 7 P.M.

02.7   The Florida Traders Auction Barn is on the left. The auction every Saturday at 7 P.M. draws a big crowd.

03.3   Old Habits Restaurant and Lounge is on the left.
The Battle of Okeechobee monument is on the left.

BATTLE OF OKEECHOBEE
The Battle of Okeechobee, which brought attention to the previously little-known lake, was fought near here on Christmas Day, 1837 (see p. 16).

04.4   Pam's Place, on the left, has pizza, beer, and wine. Joyce Williams' Taxidermy is also on left.

04.6   Nubbin Slough Road.
<u>Lake Access</u>:   The paved road to the right leads to floodgates on the slough and over the Hoover Dike into a parking area with a public boat ramp for launching directly into Lake Okeechobee. There is also a boat ramp into Nubbin Slough. The area around the floodgates is a popular fishing spot. A stand of Australian pine (casuarina) can be seen on the inside of Hoover Dike just to the west of Nubbin Slough.

04.7   Nubbin Slough.

04.8   Upthegrove Beach: A small community of mobile homes, RV resorts, fishing camps, and private homes.

05.0   Ancient Oaks RV Resort is on the left. It is one of the highest-rated resorts in the area. Condominiums are also available.

05.8   The Real Life Children's Ranch is on the left.

06.5   Junction of U.S. Route 441/State Route 98 and State Route 15A.
Continue east on U.S. Route 441/State Route 98.

08.3   A shell road leads to the right.
<u>Lake Access</u>: Henry Creek. The narrow shell road to the right leads to a small lock on the Hoover Dike. There is a boat ramp into the rim canal.

09.9   Junction U.S. Route 441/State Route 98 and State Route 15B.

Barlow Family Restaurant is on the right. It has good family food.

Continue east on U.S. Route 441/State Route 98

11.4   Blue Cypress Golf and RV Resort is on the left.

12.1   Martin County line. Much of the highway here is lined with Brazilian pepper.

14.7   J&S Trailer Park is on the right.

Lake Access: Chancey Bay. Adjacent to the J&S Trailer Park a service road leads over the Hoover Dike to Pump Station S-135. A public boat ramp extends into the rim canal.

16.8   Sugarcane fields begin to appear on the left.

21.6   Port Mayaca.

Lake Access: A paved road ahead and to the right leads to the Port Mayaca Lock and floodgates. One can drive to the top of the Hoover Dike for a great view of Lake Okeechobee. A public boat ramp here provides access into the St. Lucie Canal. The banks of the canal are a popular fishing spot.

PORT MAYACA
This small community, once considered a potential boom town location when the St. Lucie canal opened in 1921, has some elegant homes along the highway (see pp. 106-107).

22.6   The center of the high bridge over the Okeechobee Waterway/St. Lucie Canal. This point also marks the southeastern end of the large rim canal which circles the northern and northeastern shores of Lake Okeechobee. Before reaching the Okeechobee Waterway the rim canal dead-ends, and there is no access into the waterway or into Lake Okeechobee from the rim canal at this point.

ST. LUCIE CANAL

Thousands of commercial and pleasure boats pass through the lock and traverse this canal each year. The St. Lucie Canal was used as a hiding place for freighters and oil barges during World War II when these craft were subject to German U-boat attacks in the coastal waters of the Atlantic.

23.0   Junction of U.S. Route 441/State Route 98 and State Route 76.

Lake Access: Turn right on State Route 76 and proceed a short distance to a paved road to left that leads to the Hoover Dike and the Port Mayaca lock and flood-gates. One can drive to the top of the Hoover Dike for a great view of Lake Okeechobee. A public boat ramp provides access into the St. Lucie Canal. This side of the canal is also a popular fishing spot.

State Route 76 leads ten miles east, past the Port Mayaca Cemetery (see p. 107), to Indiantown. Indiantown is a residential and industrial community of about five thousand people that gets an additional two thousand snowbirds in the winter. Local or nearby special points of interest in Indiantown include the Seminole Inn, Owens Grove, Payson Park, the Barley Barber Swamp, Indiantown Marina, the Dupuis Wildlife and Environmental Area, and the J. W. Corbett Wildlife Management Area (see p. 112).

Along State Route 76 to the east of Port Mayaca are large orange groves, which are an indication of the higher and sandier ground in this area in contrast to the black muck soil in the lower swamp land. Approximately twelve miles due south of Indiantown, on similar high and sandy ground, is a large prehistoric site known as Big Mound, or Big Mound City. Preliminary archaeological work done here suggests the mounds were occupied long before Europeans arrived in Florida. The Big Mound site is not open to the public.

Continue southeast on U.S. Route 441/State Route 98

24.5 Palm Beach County line. The route passes through mainly cane country with an occasional vegetable plot or small citrus grove.

25.1 Railroad crossing.

27.5 Canal. Entering Sand Cut, a small agricultural community. The canal is a popular fishing spot.

31.0 A sugarcane field station of the U.S. Department of Agriculture, Agriculture Research Service, is on the left. Information and brochures on sugarcane and other crops are available to the public.

31.3 Canal Point: A small community. This is the point where the old Connors Highway from West Palm Beach reached Lake Okeechobee.
<u>Lake Access:</u> On the right is a town park with a picnic area. The road leads over the Hoover Dike to a parking area with more picnic facilities and a boat ramp for launching directly into Lake Okeechobee. This area provides a fine scenic view. A plaque in the park honors W. J. Connors, the man who built the highway (see p.113).

CONNORS HIGHWAY

The Connors Highway, which extends to the southeast, parallels the West Palm Beach Canal and leads to West Palm Beach, some forty miles east. The other part of this historic highway is that portion of U.S. Route 441/State Route 98 extending from here back to Okeechobee.

31.6 West Palm Beach Canal (L-10) is another popular fishing spot. The road that heads due east immediately across the canal is the old Connors Highway.

Proceeding east on the Connors Highway (which soon intersects and becomes State Route 98) about one and a half miles east on the right is the giant U.S.

Sugar's Bryant Mill Refinery. Another big plant, Osceola Farm Company Refinery, is on the left about six and a half miles down the road. This is a fairly rough road with a lot of truck traffic during cane harvesting, but it is an interesting short tour of cane country. About sixteen miles from Canal Point the road intersects U.S. Route 441, which heads east. The cane fields end gradually a few miles east of this point. Five miles east of the intersection, on U.S. Route 441, is Lion Country Safari (see pp. 101-102). Further down U.S. Route 441, where the road turns and heads due south, is the Loxahatchee Wildlife Refuge (see p. 102).

Continue south on U.S. Route 441/State Route 98.

31.7　Junction of U.S. Route 441 and State Route 98. At this point State Route 98 leaves U.S. Route 441 and heads due east to connect with the Connors Highway.

Proceed southeast on U.S. Route 441.

Majestic royal palms line the right side of the highway as U.S. Route 441 turns right (south) and heads toward Pahokee.

ROYAL PALM
The bright green shaft, up to three or four feet long, which separates the top of the light-colored trunk from the bottom of the fronds is actually the oldest leaf in the crown.

31.9　Jones Fish House is on the right (see p. 113).
32.3　Pahokee city limit.
32.7　Railroad crossing. The road to the left leads to U.S. Sugar's giant Bryant Mill.

PAHOKEE
Pahokee, one of the last towns to be settled in the Okeechobee area, established its post office in 1916 and was incorporated in 1922. (see pp. 104-106).

33.0   Railroad crossing and junction of County Route 729 with U.S. 441.

33.4   Beautiful royal palms line both sides of highway.

34.5   Elks lodge is on the right. Lunch is served here daily and it is open to the public.

34.9   End of Leg 1: Downtown Pahokee at the junction of County Route 715 and U.S. Route 441.

The Pahokee Chamber of Commerce is on the right. <u>Lake Access:</u> The road to the right leads over the Hoover Dike to Pahokee Marina & Campground.

PAHOKEE MARINA & CAMPGROUND
Commercial boats moored here offer dining, lake cruises and fishing trips. The view of Lake Okeechobee is great and sunsets from this vantage point are outstanding (see p. 104).

EAST SIDE   Bed race at Pahokee during Grassy Water Festival, November, 1995

Leg 2: Pahokee to Moore Haven: 46 miles

00.0   Starting point: The Pahokee Chamber of Commerce on U.S. Route 441/State Route 15 in downtown Pahokee.

       Turn left and continue south on U.S. Route 441/State Route 15.

ALTERNATE ROUTE

This route is closest to Lake Okeechobee and it passes through a beautiful residential section of Pahokee, along a road lined with many royal palm trees. Most of the residences are on the right, near the Hoover Dike; farmland (mostly cane) is on the left.

00.0   Starting point: Same as the main route, at the Chamber of Commerce on U.S. Route 441/State Route 15 in downtown Pahokee .

       Turn left on 441/15, then right in one block (at the light) on County Route 715 (Bacom Point Road). Proceed south.

00.2   The Pahokee Post Office is on the right.

00.3   Loula V. York Memorial Library and a park are on the right.

00.9   Pioneer Park is on the right.

PIONEER PARK
Thirty-four adults and children, victims of the 1928 hurricane, lie here in a mass grave. Their names are listed on a memorial plaque (see p.106).

02.7   Canal, floodgate/Pump Station No. 10 on Hoover Dike.

Leaving Pahokee.

03.2   Duncan Padgett Park and athletic fields are on the left.

03.4   Palm Beach County's Glades Airport is on the right.

04.1   Small canal. The road to the right leads, after a short distance, to the top of the Hoover Dike and the No. 12A pump station. There is a good view of Lake Okeechobee and Kreamer Island from the top of the dike. This area has been used as a boat launch directly into Lake Okeechobee, but it is primitive and not recommended for anything other than a light boat or canoe. It is an unofficial lake access point.

04.8   The highway now runs adjacent to Hoover Dike. The inside of dike is lined with exotic Australian pine (casuarina).

06.1   Palm Beach County, Paul Rardin Park.
Lake Access: The road into Paul Rardin Park leads over the Hoover Dike to a double boat ramp for launching directly into Lake Okeechobee. The Okeechobee Waterway lies immediately offshore, and large boats and ships pass by here.

06.3   A small canal with a floodgate on the Hoover Dike.

PAUL RARDIN PARK

Paul Rardin Park is a lovely site with covered picnic tables, a pavilion with a grill, a small playground with swings, and restrooms. The entrance road is lined with royal palms. Strangler figs are entwined on most of the oak trees that were originally planted in the park. The strangler is one of southern Florida's most unusual trees. After making its appearance, it doesn't actually strangle its victim, but rather slowly takes over the nutrient system, and this eventually kills the host tree. There is no overnight camping or parking here, but it is a delightful spot for a family picnic or reunion.

07.9   Junction of County Route 715 with Hooker Highway. This road, which leads right one and one-tenth mile to the Hoover Dike and an old floodgate, is strictly a service road. There is no access to the dike or to the lake.
       Continue south on County Route 715.
08.2   West Technical Education Center is on the left. The casuarina-lined Hoover Dike lies about a mile to the right.
08.9   WSWN Radio Station is on the left.
09.5   Entering Belle Glade.
09.8   Entering Chosen.

CHOSEN

Chosen and Belle Glade were once separate towns, each with their own post office, but eventually Chosen became a small suburb within the city of Belle Glade. The Chosen Mounds, ancient native structures, are near here but are not open to the public.

10.1   Hillsboro Canal, L-14/junction of County Route 715 and County Route 717.
       <u>Lake Access</u> to Belle Glade Marina Campground is to the right.
       Continue south on County Route 715.
10.9   Railroad crossing.
11.4   Palm Beach Community College is on the right.
11.8   Glades Pioneer Regional Park is on the left.
12.3   Junction of County Route 715 and State Route 80. Hoover Dike is now in the far distance to the right, as marked by the line of casuarina trees.
                    End of alternate route.

00.1   Pam's Seafood Restaurant & Market is on the right. It is one of the best places in the lake area to try Okeechobee catfish.

01.3   Leaving Pahokee.

01.4   Railroad crossing and junction of U.S. Route 441/State Route 15 with County Routes 717 and 729. County Route 717 goes east; County Route 729 goes northeast.

    The Pahokee watertower is on the left

    Proceed south on U.S. Route 441/State Route 15.

    The highway is elevated about ten feet above the old swamp beds, which are now planted largely in sugarcane with a few vegetable and cornfields. Hoover Dike lies about two and a half miles west.

08.0   Junction with Hooker Highway. Hooker Highway heads west and US Route 441 goes east.

    Proceed straight ahead on State Route 15.

08.1   The Belle Glade Work Center, part of the Florida Department of Agriculture and Consumer Services, Division of Forestry, is on the left.

08.5   The Glades Correctional Institution/Workcamp is on the left.

09.0   Junction of State Route 15 and Curlee Road. Curlee Road to the left leads to the huge Sugar Cane Grower's Cooperative sugar mill and the adjacent Great Lakes Chemical Corporation plant.

09.4   Railroad crossing.

09.9   Belle Glade city limit.

    Belle Glade Airport is on the left.

10.0   Junction of State Route 15 and NW Ave. L.

    <u>Lake Access:</u> Turn right on NW Ave. L and go one mile

---

SUGAR CANE GROWER'S COOPERATIVE SUGAR MILL

This huge mill is operated by fifty-six small- to medium-size sugarcane farms in the Everglades Agricultural Area. The cooperative harvests, processes, and markets the sugar. Visitors can stop by the mill office to receive brochures and other information. The cooperative will also send an information package and loan a video to an individual or a group. Write Sugar Cane Growers Cooperative of Florida, P.O. Box 666, Belle Glade, FL 33430, (407) 996-5556.

west to County Route 715. Turn left and go one-tenth mile to County Route 717. Turn right and proceed two and two-tenths miles along the Hillsboro Canal to Belle Glade Marina Campground. This route passes through a residential area, cane fields, and past the eighteen-hole Belle Glade Municipal Golf Course. The front nine holes are on the right side of the road and the back nine are a little farther down the road on the left, adjacent to the Drawbridge Cafe and Rusty Anchor Lounge. The road continues over the Hoover Dike and over a hand-operated wooden swing bridge over the Okeechobee Waterway to the marina/campground. This is said to be one of only three similar hand-operated swing bridges in the United States.

10.7   Hillsboro Canal, L-14 and the junction of State Route 15 and County Route 717.

Continue straight ahead on State Route 15.

The Everglades Research Station, University of Florida, Institute of Food and Agricultural Science, lies two and a half miles east of here at 3200 East Palm Beach Road. To get there, turn left on the south side of the canal (on East Canal Street). Information about agriculture in the Everglades is available to the public at the office of the research station.

For a drive through the heart of cane country, continue straight ahead past the research station on the paved road that parallels the Hillsboro Canal. Turn right three and a half miles east of the research station on the paved road that continues to parallel the canal. The pavement goes for another twelve and two-tenths miles where it ends and a shell road continues. This is Brown's Farm Road which eventually leads to a wildlife management area. The road has very heavy truck traffic during cane harvesting season.

11.0   Junction of State Route 15 and County Route 880E.

Continue straight ahead on State Route 15.

11.1   The Belle Glade Chamber of Commerce, Library, and the Lawrence E. Will Museum is on the right. The City Hall is behind these buildings.

11.7   The National Guard Armory is on the right.

11.9   The Glades General Hospital is on the left.

12.1   Junction of State Route 15, County Route 827A, and State Route 80.
      Turn right and proceed west on State Route 80.

13.2   Junction of State Route 80 and County Route 715
      Continue straight ahead on State Route 80.

14.4   Entering South Bay, "A Special Place We Call Home."

14.7   L-20 Canal.
      The Post Office is on the right

14.9   Junction of State Route 80 and U.S. Route 27.
      Bear right on U.S. Route 27/State Route 80 toward Clewiston.
      U.S. Route 27 to the left leads four miles to Okeelanta, one of the first settlements on the south side of Lake Okeechobee, and another thirty-seven miles across cane country and the Everglades to Alligator Alley (Interstate 75).

15.2   The Okeechobee Inn is on the left. It is one of the better motels in the area.

15.3   Railroad crossing.

16.6   South Bay Campground, Palm Beach County, Parks and Recreation Department/South Bay is on the right. Lake Access: Follow the campground road over the Hoover Dike to multiple public ramps that allow boat launching directly into Lake Okeechobee. The Okeechobee Waterway is immediately in front of the ramps.
      The Hoover Dike now lies adjacent to the highway for most of the way to Clewiston.

21.3   Lake Harbor.

21.6   Miami Canal (L-25), pump station and floodgates on the Hoover Dike are to the right. A historical marker with information about the old lock is to the left.

21.8   John Stretch Park on right.

Lake Access: Take the road through the park and over the Hoover Dike to a primitive ramp for launching boats directly into Lake Okeechobee. The Okeechobee Waterway is immediately in front of the launch site.

21.9   A water tower is on the left.

27.2   The Crooked Hook RV Resort is on the left.

27.8   Hendry County line.

29.9   The Everglades Sugar Refinery is down a road to the left.

30.0   Clewiston (see pp. 93-95). The U.S. Army Corps of Engineers offices is on the right.

Highway crosses a large canal. This canal leads a short distance to a lock on the Hoover Dike.

30.2   Francisco Street.

Lake Access: Turn right on Francisco Street and proceed seven-tenths mile past the BPOE Lodge, Roland Martin Marina/Hotel, and Angler's Marina & Motel over the Hoover Dike into Hoover Memorial Park. There are picnic tables and public boat ramps for launching directly into Lake Okeechobee. The Okeechobee Waterway lies immediately offshore. Just before the Hoover Dike, there is a large parking lot and multiple boat ramps where boats can be put into the rim canal. However, this requires going through the S-310 lock to get into Lake Okeechobee. The Wayside RV Park here is operated by the town. There is no overnighting in Hoover Memorial Park.

30.4   The Old South Bar-B-Que Ranch is on the left offers barbecue and country food. It's worth a stop to see the many antiques displayed in the restaurant.

30.9   The Clewiston Inn is on the right (see pp. 94-95).

For a drive through a beautiful residential area, turn right on Royal Palm Avenue at the Clewiston Inn and proceed north. There are municipal tennis courts on the left just after turning down the avenue.

31.0 The Clewiston City Hall and the Clewiston Museum are to the left.

31.1 U.S. Sugar Corporate Headquarters are on the right; W. C. Owens Avenue is to the left. U.S. Sugar's giant Clewiston Mill is one mile south on W. C. Owens Avenue (County Route 832).

An interesting drive can be taken from here south through the heart of sugarcane country. Turn left (east) at the Clewiston Mill on State Route 832 and proceed two miles to a "T" in the road. Turn right (on State Route 835), then follow this main road (past the Evercane Sugarcane Mill on the right about five miles from Clewiston) thirty-one miles to its intersection with State Route 833. (Note: this route (S.R. 835) turns west at a right angle three times and south at a right angle twice. Also, it is poorly marked and incorrectly labeled on Florida's official state highway map. However, if the main pavement is followed, there should be no serious problem in reaching State Route 833). Turn left on 833 and proceed six miles to the Big Cypress Seminole Indian Reservation (see p. 96). The route from Clewiston to the reservation passes through cane fields and then a relatively rugged area of cattle ranches, fallow ground, some large citrus groves, and an occasional vegetable farm, collectively known as the Devil's Garden.

A right turn instead of a left on State Route 833, would lead one about thirty miles to Immokalee, where there is the Seminole Gaming Palace and the nearby Audubon Society's Corkscrew Swamp Sanctuary (see p. 97). The gaming palace lies on County Road 846, six-tenths of a mile south of its junction with State Route 29. The Sunniland Oil Field (see pp. 97-98) is a few miles south of Immokalee.

There is a small park, Oil Well Park, just off the west side of Route 29, one and four-tenths miles south of the junction of Route 29 and County Road 858. It contains a picnic area, an old pumping unit, and a plaque dedicated to the Sunniland Oil Field discovery.

31.3   Hendry General Hospital is on the left.

31.6   The Clewiston News office is on the right.

31.7   The Clewiston Post Office is on the left. The Hoover Dike now lies about two miles to the right (north).

32.5   Railroad crossing and junction of U.S. Route 27/State Route 80 and the road to Harlem, a small community southwest of Clewiston. During World War II, Royal Air Force cadets from Britain trained at nearby Riddle Airfield.

Proceed west on U.S. Route 27/State Route 80.

33.6   Junction of U.S. Route 27/State Route 80 and County Route 720.

ALTERNATE ROUTE

This alternate route goes closer to the Hoover Dike and passes through the heart of sugarcane country.

00.0   Starting point: Junction of U.S. Route 27/State Route 80 and County Route 720. Turn right (north) on County Route 720.

00.1   KOA Kampground is on the right.

00.7   Railroad crossing

02.8   Service road to the right leads to Pump Station S-4 on the Hoover Dike.

03.7   Junction of County Route 720 and Griffin Road.
Lake Access: Turn right on Griffin Road and proceed seven-tenths of a mile to Uncle Joe's Fish Camp adjacent to the Hoover Dike. It is the only private camp on Lake Okeechobee with its own access road over the Hoover Dike. This road leads to a single boat ramp

that allows launching directly into Lake Okeechobee. The Okeechobee Waterway lies immediately offshore. The camp also provides lakeside dockage. A $3 fee is charged for using the boat ramp.

09.0   Railroad crossing. A watertower is on the left.

10.3   Junction of County Route 720 and U.S. Route 27/State Route 80.

> End of alternate route.

Proceed west on U.S. Route 27/State Route 80. For the next eight miles, the highway passes through poorer soil. Here there is less sugarcane and an increasing amount of beef cattle pastureland, citrus groves, and some vegetable plots. However, there are still some sizable plots of cane along this stretch of the highway.

40.2   Junction of U.S. Route 27 and State Route 80. State Route 80 heads west to La Belle and Ft. Myers.
> Proceed on U.S. Route 27, which turns north.

41.2   Glades County line.
> Vast cane fields reappear in this area. The Hoover Dike lies in the distance to the right, marked by a line of Australian pine trees (casuarina).

45.5   End of the four-lane highway. Two lanes continue to Moore Haven.

45.9   Caloosahatchee River, the west link of the Cross Florida/Okeechobee Waterway.
Lake Access: The paved road to the right, just before the river, leads eight-tenths of a mile over the Hoover Dike and into the Alvin L. Ward Sr. Memorial Public Park of Glades County. This park does not allow overnight camping, but it has covered picnic tables, a pavilion, playground, restrooms, and five ramps for launching boats directly into Lake Okeechobee. There is also an airboat ramp. The Okeechobee Waterway

lies immediately offshore. The area around the lock is a popular fishing spot for snook and other fish.

46.0   Moore Haven.

End of Leg 2.

Leg 3: Moore Haven to Okeechobee: 36.8 miles

00.0   Starting point: Moore Haven town line, west bank of the Caloosahatchee River, on U.S. Route 27.

Proceed west on U.S. Route 27, entering Moore Haven.

00.1   Rice Motel: A nice place to stay in Moore Haven.

The Moore Haven Restaurant, across the street on the right side of U.S. Route 27, offers family food.

Lake Access: Turn right on 1st Street (next to the Rice Hotel) and proceed one-tenth mile north to a public boat ramp on the right. This ramp allows launching boats into a small canal which, after a short distance, leads into the Caloosahatchee River. Another three-tenth mile north on 1st Street is the Moore Haven Yacht Club on the right. After another one-tenth mile north the road comes to a "T." The road to right leads to the Sportsman's Marina and Campground and the Moore Haven lock.

The Moore Haven Yacht Club, a privately owned RV resort located directly on the banks of the Caloosahatchee River, is operated by Camper Clubs of America. Although it is a member park, the public is welcome. There is no boat ramp, but guests can use nearby ramps located just outside the park.

The Sportsman's Marina and Campground is a full-service marina and RV resort, owned and operated by Thousand Adventures. The campsite, leased from the Army Corps of Engineers, is over the Hoover Dike and is, therefore, one of the few right on the lakefront.

Boats can be launched here, for a small fee, directly into Lake Okeechobee. Rentals are also available.

MOORE HAVEN LOCK
The Moore Haven Lock, on the Cross-Florida/Okeechobee Waterway, is one of the two largest lock s on the lake.

00.2 The Dairy King Restaurant, on the right, offers Chinese food.

00.5 The Glades County Courthouse is on the left.

00.9 The Moore Haven Chamber of Commerce is on the left. Directly behind the chamber of commerce is the Bronson Arena.

A Subway Restaurant is located behind the Texaco Station across the street.

BRONSON ARENA
The Bronson arena is the site of the "Cattlemen's Cracker Days" Rodeo, held in Moore Haven the first Saturday in October.

01.0 The Glades Inn and Restaurant is on the right. This facility underwent extensive renovation in early 1996.

02.0 Junction of U.S. 27 and State Route 78.

Turn right onto State Route 78 and proceed north toward Okeechobee.

The road straight ahead, U.S. Route 27/State Route 78, leads to Palmdale and past two interesting attractions, Gatorama and Cypress Kneeland (see pp. 118-119). Also, four miles down this road, State Route 78 leaves U.S. Route 27 and goes to Ortona where the Ortona Indian Mounds and the Ortona Lock Recreation Area are located (see pp. 117-118).

The Ortona Indian Mounds are just off State Route 78, eight miles west of the junction of U.S. Route 27 and State Route 78. About seven-tenths of a mile west of the Ortona Mounds on State Road 78 is the junction with State Road 78A. The Ortona Lock Recreation Area is one and nine-tenths miles south of this junction on Route 78A.

02.3   The Moore Haven Correctional Institution is on the right.

At this point the Hoover Dike lies about two miles to the right and is marked by the long line of Australian pines (casuarina) inside the dike. The area between State Route 78 and the dike is largely beef cattle pasturage, while the area to the left of the road is mostly sugarcane fields.

03.3   Railroad crossing.

05.7   L-41 canal with a small floodgate into Lake Okeechobee. The Hoover Dike is now adjacent to the road.

06.2   The exotic tree melaleuca begins to line the inside of the Hoover Dike.

The large mound to the left of the road is not an ancient Indian mound, but an old Moore Haven landfill.

The many palm trees seen scattered along the highway from here to Okeechobee are nearly all sabal (cabbage) palms, the state tree of Florida. The older trees are mostly smooth-trunked while the younger ones may retain "boots," the bases of their fallen fronds.

08.1   Nicodemus Slough and floodgate into Lake Okeechobee.

08.3   Nicodemus Slough Park. On the left is a little park with a small lake, boat ramp, fishing pier, and a picnic area. The park, a Save Our Rivers Project managed by the South Florida Water Management District, was opened in early 1996.

08.4 The Hoover Dike crosses the road and heads west away from Lake Okeechobee. The road now continues down into the marshy area of the northwestern part of Lake Okeechobee, inside the Hoover Dike.

08.5 Large canal.

08.6 Sportsman's Village access area to the right.

Lake Access: The Sportsman's Village access area has a small parking lot with a picnic area and a ramp for launching boats into the canal, which extends east a short distance into Lake Okeechobee.

10.3 The Vance W. Whidden Recreation Area and Curry Island are on the right. A primitive road leads into the recreational area and to Curry Island. This area is normally closed due to problems with illegal dumping in the past. One needs a permit to enter.

11.1 Fisheating Creek (see pp. 119-120).

11.5 Entering Lakeport.

Lake Access: The small park on the right has picnic tables and a boat ramp that leads into Fisheating Creek, which in turn leads, after a short distance, directly into Lake Okeechobee (no locks).

Lakeport marks the approximate northwestern limit of the sugarcane fields. Farmlands from here to Okeechobee are largely beef cattle pasturage, much of it owned or leased by by Lykes Bros., Inc.

11.6 The Hoover Dike again crosses the highway and extends west. The highway passes over the dike and once more the Hoover Dike is between the highway and Lake Okeechobee.

11.9 Junction of State Route 78 and Glades County Route 74. County Route 74 to the left leads to a residential and RV resort area of Lakeport. This road extends west only a few miles and then dead ends. The Lakeport Community Center, where the Sour Orange Festival is held, is one mile from here. To reach the center, drive a half mile down Route 74, turn right at the water tower, and proceed a half mile.

12.9   Junction of State Route 78 and Glades County Route 721.

ALTERNATE ROUTE

This alternate route goes closer to the lake than does the main road, State Route 78. It leads to a small residential area with several RV resorts, fishing camps, and marinas.

00.0   Starting point: Junction of State Route 78 and County Route 721.

   Turn right off State Route 78 and proceed northeast on County Route 721.

00.6   Junction of County Route 721 and pump station road.

   The pump station road (to the right) leads, after a short distance, to the Hoover Dike, the S-131 Pump Station, and a small lock. There is no boat ramp; however, a small boat or canoe can be launched into the rim canal.

00.8   Big Bass Lodge and Guide Service is on the right. The lock and pump station can be seen to the right.

02.2   The Calusa Lodge is on the left.

02.4   Junction of County Route 721 and State Route 78.
                End of alternate route.

13.2   North Lake Estates, a large RV resort, is on the right.

13.6   Elderberry Cottage Restaurant and Gift Shop, on the left, offers family food. "Best Food On The Lake."

14.9   The Calusa Lodge, on the right, offers food and weekend entertainment. It's worth a stop if only to see the big collection of mounted Okeechobee bass and other game specimens.

15.0   Junction of State Route 78 and County Route 721. Continue straight ahead on State Route 78.

15.4   Harney Pond Canal.

The Harney Pond Canal is one of the largest drainage canals that leads into Lake Okeechobee. The Hoover Dike crosses the road on both sides of the canal and extends for several miles to the west.

Lake Access: Just across the canal, the paved and shell road to the right leads to the Margaret Van de Velde Park, Harney Pond Recreation and Picnic Area. There is a large parking area with three boat ramps and small fishing piers. Two of the ramps lead into Harney Pond Canal; the other leads into a small canal on the opposite side of the road. These canals lead directly into Lake Okeechobee (no locks). At the end of the park is a picnic area and a boardwalk that leads to an elevated platform with a great view of the marshy western shore of Lake Okeechobee. This is an excellent spot for birdwatching. There is also a small parking area and boat ramp into the Harney Pond Canal on the northwest corner of the canal, just off the highway.

15.5   Junction of State Route 78 and Glades County Route 721. County Route 721 leads northwest to the Brighton Indian Reservation, which holds a festival each year on President's Day weekend.

Lakeport Lodge and Restaurant and the Duck Pub are on the right.

Glenn Hunter's RV Park-Store and Guide Service is on the left.

16.5   Junction of State Route 78 and Dyess Road.

Lake Access: Turn right off State Route 78 onto Dyess Road, which leads over the rim canal and the dike to Bare Beach. There is a large parking area with three ramps for launching boats directly into Lake Okeechobee. A small sand beach area allows additional boat launching. Some boaters simply leave their trailers submerged in the water off this beach until they return from hunting or fishing trips. A long line of melaleuca trees block the lake view off Bare Beach. Just before reaching the rim canal from the highway, there is a primitive area where a light boat can be launched into a small canal that leads into the rim canal.

17.9   Leaving Lakeport.

The highway from here to Buckhead Ridge (about twelve miles) passes through one of the most desolate areas around Lake Okeechobee. Only a few scattered ranch houses are seen. Sabal palms and Brazilian pepper trees line much of the highway. This is mostly beef cattle grazing land, although an occasional small orange grove may be seen. The Hoover Dike now lies to the east, a quarter mile or more away in places.

20.1   Junction of State Route 78 and paved road.

The paved road to the right is a service road that leads onto the Hoover Dike to the S-121 Pump Station.

Continue straight ahead on State Route 78.

23.0   Indian Prairie Canal.

Here the dike comes up both sides of the large Indian Prairie Canal and then extends west for several miles along the sides of the canal. This allows the canal to feed directly into Lake Okeechobee.

Lake Access: The shell road to the right and adjacent to the Indian Prairie Canal on its southwest bank leads a half mile to a boat ramp into the canal (which then leads a short distance directly into Lake Okeechobee) and to the Indian Prairie Campground, a primitive RV/tent campground directly on the canal. There is no charge for staying at this campground. A large group camping area lies further down this road. Reservations and a permit are required for the group area and there is a $25 charge per group. The campground is operated by the U.S. Army Corps of Engineers. Call (941) 983-8101.

29.7 Entering Buckhead Ridge.

Junction of State Route 78 and Glades County Route 78B (Access Road). Although this is called "Access Road," there is no access for boaters. Instead, this is a service road to the Buckhead Ridge Lock and Pump Station.

ALTERNATE ROUTE

This route, passing closer to the Hoover Dike than State Route 78, goes through part of the community of Buckhead Ridge. A turn off the alternate route will also take one across the rim canal to a small lock on the dike.

00.0 Starting point: Junction of State Route 78 and County Route 78B.
Turn right off State Route 78 and proceed east on County Route 78B (Access Road).

00.6 The road straight ahead leads to the pump station and lock. Turn left over a small canal and proceed north on County Route 78B through a residential and RV area.

00.7 The Buckhead Marina and Restaurant is on the right. The restaurant is open from 6 A.M. to 2 P.M., catering to the early shift of anglers.

01.7 Bear right on Linda Gardens Road.

02.7 Junction of County Route 78B with State Route 78.
End of alternate route.

31.3 The Buckhead Ridge water tower is on the right.

31.5 The Buckhead Ridge Moose Lodge is on the right.

31.6 Cliff Pearce Park and the Buckhead Ridge Community Center are on the right.

31.9   Leaving Buckhead Ridge.

32.0   The Hoover Dike crosses the road and trends east-west along the west bank of the Kissimmee River.

32.1   Kissimmee River.

This location is less than a mile from the mouth of the Kissimmee, where it enters Lake Okeechobee.

Lake Access: There are several places for access into the Kissimmee River in this vicinity. On the northwest corner of the bridge is a primitive access area where a small boat can be launched. Across the river, there are launch sites at Okee-Tantie Recreation Area on the right and directly across the highway at the C. Scott Driver Recreation Area.

KISSIMMEE RIVER
The Kissimmee River is the major stream that flows into Lake Okeechobee. River otters are common along this stream.

32.2   Swamplands Tours. Just over the river, on the left side, is Swampland Tours. These highly popular tours are given through the Audubon Reserve on the west side of Lake Okeechobee. This is an enjoyable way to get better acquainted with the flora and fauna of the region.

32.3   Okee-Tantie Recreation Area is on the right.

Lake Access: The Okee-Tantie Recreation Area has multiple ramps for launching boats into the Kissimmee River. This beautiful park is operated by Okeechobee County and, in addition to the boat ramps, has a bait and tackle shop, RV and tent campsites, and Lightsey's Seafood Restaurant.

32.4   Mr. G's RV Resort is on the right. This is one of the few private campgrounds inside the Hoover Dike.

32.5   The top of the Hoover Dike.

Lake Access: The paved road to the left on the side of the dike (SW 99th Drive) leads to the C. Scott Driver Jr. Recreation Area. This has a large parking area and a double boat ramp leading into the Kissimmee River. A short distance down SW 99th Drive is the Old River Run RV Park, another private campground inside the dike.

36.7   Jaycee Park is on the right.

Lake Access: The road to the right leads over the rim canal and the Hoover Dike to the large Jaycee Park, which has a beach, fishing pier, and a double boat ramp leading directly into Lake Okeechobee.

36.8   Junction of State Route 78 and U.S. 441/ State Route 98.

End of Leg 3 and end of driving tour.

APPENDIX 2

Hiking/Biking Tour Around Lake Okeechobee

On the Florida National Scenic Trail,
Okeechobee Segment, on top of the
Herbert Hoover Dike (Clockwise)

*H*iking and biking along the top of the Herbert Hoover Dike offers an unparalleled panoramic view of a natural wonderland. While visitors who drive around the lake in an automobile without taking side trips to access points may not even see the lake, hikers and bicycle riders view it all — the lake and its wildlife on one side and the countryside with its flora, fauna, and culture on the other side.

For some, the route may be a journey of nearly 110 miles to be made as quickly as possible, simply to meet the challenge of doing it. Others will take bird, plant, animal, and fossil lists, and try to observe and identify many of the myriad of species along the way. In either case, the journey provides good exercise and an opportunity for an unusual learning experience.

Organized trips are taken around the lake. For example, a "Big O" Bike Tour and a "Big O" Hike are held yearly. These user-friendly trips have vehicles to pick up tired participants, who can get as much or as little exercise as they want.

Food and refreshments can be obtained at several localities by exiting the dike trail for a short excursion into a nearby

Hike/Bike Tour Trip Legs

1. Jaycee Park, Okeechobee to Taylor Creek: 2.2 miles
2. Taylor Creek to Nubbin Slough: 2.5 miles
3. Nubbin Slough to Henry Creek: 3.5 miles
4. Henry Creek to Chancey Bay: 6.7 miles
5. Chancey Bay to Port Mayaca: 7.6 miles
6. Port Mayaca to Canal Point: 9.0 miles
7. Canal Point to Pahokee: 3.6 miles
8. Pahokee to Paul Rardin Park: 6.3 miles
9. Paul Rardin Park to Belle Glade Marina Campground: 3.6 miles
10. Belle Glade Marina Campground to South Bay Campground: 2.0 miles
11. South Bay Campground to John Stretch Park: 5.2 miles
12. John Stretch Park to Clewiston: 8.4 miles
13. Clewsiton to Moore Haven: 12.6 miles
14. Moore Haven to Sportsman's Village Park: 7.0 miles
15. Sportsman's Village Park to Lakeport: 2.8 miles
16. Lakeport to Margaret Van de Velde Park: 4.3 miles
17. Margaret van de Velde Park to Bare Beach: 1.0 mile
18. Bare Beach to Indian Praire Canal: 7.2 miles
19. Indian Prairie Canal to Kissimmee River: 9.5 miles
20. Kissimmee River to Jaycee Park, Okeechobee: 4.3 miles

town or to an adjacent campground/marina. Several places around the dike trail, marked by signs, are designated as primitive campsites by the Florida Trail Association. Most of these campsites are pointed out in this log. Visitors can also stay at improved campsites in private or public parks or at motels.

When the master plan for the scenic trail is completed, there will be public restrooms spaced around the trail. Currently, these facilities are limited to the Pahokee Marina & Campground, Paul Rardin Park, Belle Glade Marina Campground, South Bay Campground, John Stretch Park, parks in Clewiston and Moore Haven, Margaret Van de Velde Park, and the Okee-Tantie Recreation Area. The remoteness of much of the rest of the area, however, allows one to attend to such necessary matters in relative privacy.

Hikers and bikers should carry food, water, sunscreen, and insect repellent. This tour gives azimuths along the route, and an inexpensive pocket compass will allow the traveler to remain oriented. Although one cannot get lost on the trail, it can be fun to use azimuths.

An azimuth is the distance in degrees from north. For example, a 90 degree azimuth is due east, a 180 degree azimuth is due south, a 270 degree azimuth is due west, and a 360 degree azimuth is due north. If a one is heading at an azimuth of 45 degrees, he or she is going northeast. An azimuth of 315 degrees is to the northwest.

To read an azimuth, position the compass so its needle points to the north reading. Then, sight over the compass in the direction in which you are going and read the number of degrees that the compass indicates for that bearing.

The mileage for this tour was measured by bicycle computer. For convenience, the tour is broken down into twenty legs, from one public access point to another. Thus, a hiker or biker can go to an access point, then hike or bike to another access point where a meeting can be arranged with a support vehicle. The shortest leg, Leg 17 from Margaret Van de Velde Park in Lakeport to Bare Beach, on the western side of

Lake Okeechobee, is just a mile; the longest, from Clewiston to Moore Haven, is twelve and six-tenths miles. Other legs vary from two miles to nine and a half miles.

Organized bicycle trips are usually broken into three segments of nearly equal length: from Okeechobee to Pahokee (35.1 miles), Pahokee to Moore Haven (38.1 miles), and from Moore Haven to Okeechobee (36.1 miles). The unofficial total for the entire tour, as measured by bicycle computer, is 109.3 miles.

This log was compiled after many trips along the levee. Each sector was traveled at least twice, some a dozen or more times. Yet each traverse seems to result in something new. For example:

- A young bald eagle (less than five years old, as she has not yet developed the characteristic white-feathered head) is seen perched on the Hoover Dike, resting between fishing forays. She takes off and swoops low over Lake Okeechobee, hits the surface, and emerges with a large fish in her talons. She flies a hundred yards and drops her lucky prey in the lake. She rests again on the levee before making another try. A more successful fisher, an osprey, flies to a high water tower to eat his catch.

- A huge, black, ropy thing ahead on the trail turns out to be an enormous water moccasin. It coils and rears back, opening a white, cotton mouth in warning. It doesn't retreat and has to be detoured around. (Don't worry, these are rarely sighted — driving in Florida traffic presents infinitely more danger.)

- In the early evening, a nine-banded armadillo comes to the top of the dike to begin his nightly digs for grubs. Raccoons begin to scramble over the dike to go to the Lake Okeechobee shore in their nocturnal search for food. Perhaps a bobcat is spotted. The Florida panther has been seen in this area. A big, sleek, black river otter scurries over the dike.

- In the daytime, the great blue heron is seen at such spaced intervals that territoriality is assumed. A group of cattle egrets leap-frog ahead of hikers and bikers. Black vultures and turkey buzzards leave their favorite roosting areas to soar above in large, circling flocks, and, occasionally, a Mexican eagle (caracara) joins them.

- The distinctive cries of a flock of black birds give away their identity — they are smooth-billed anis, a member of the cuckoo family and a bird found only in southern Florida.

- Large birds creating a ruckus along the dike ahead turn out to be four sandhill cranes, one of Florida's most beautiful, large birds.

- A huge alligator, basking in the sun near the lakeshore, watches the action through sleepy eyes.

- An exciting discovery of a different type of fossil shell is made. In some places, there may be abundant conical snail shells; in others, there may be many clam shells.

It seems visitors can find something unusual along the Hoover Dike on each trip. It grows on them, especially after they view a gorgeous sunset from atop this panoramic vantage point.

Leg 1: Jaycee Park, Okeechobee, to Taylor Creek: 2.2 miles

Leg 1 extends along a fairly densely populated sector of the greater Okeechobee area. Brazilian pepper, casuarina, and sabal palms are the predominant vegetation along the lakeshore and rim canal. There are good views of Lake Okeechobee between the taller trees.

JAYCEE PARK
(also referred to as "Lock 7," although there is no lock)
This park on the lakeshore has a good view of Lake Okeechobee.
The east end is lined with sabal palms, the official state tree of
Florida. This is a good fossil study area.

00.00   Starting point: Top of the Hoover Dike at Jaycee
        Park.

        Enter Jaycee Park from the highway one hundred
        yards west of the intersection of U.S. Route 441/State
        Route 98 and State Route 78, at the south end of
        Parrott Avenue. The road crosses a bridge over the
        rim canal and goes over the dike to the park.

        The center of Okeechobee is three miles north on
        Parrott Avenue.

        Proceed eastward on top of the Hoover Dike,
        azimuth 65 degrees.

        The rim canal bank is lined predominantly with
        Brazilian pepper trees, while the lakeshore has
        Brazilian pepper and Australian pine (casuarina)
        trees.

        There are good views of Lake Okeechobee except
        where the vista is blocked by tall casuarina.

        In the fall and winter, smoke from burning cane
        fields can be seen in the distant south and east. The
        cane country along the south shore of Lake
        Okeechobee is more than thirty miles from here.

        Numerous mobile home parks, RV resorts, and
        fishing camps are along the north bank of the rim
        canal.

        Cypress and live oak trees draped with Spanish
        moss and sabal palms are across the highway to the
        north.

00.90   The dike curves 10 degrees eastward to an azimuth
        of 75 degrees.

The Big Lake Marina is on the rim canal.

01.00   Casuarina increases along the lakefront, but there are good views of Lake Okeechobee between stands of these trees.

01.70   The Pier II/Days Inn motel is across the rim canal.

Note the cattail marshes on the north bank of the rim canal along both sides of Pier II. Similar areas around the lake were once saw grass marshes, but nutrients from runoff killed the saw grass while cattails thrive.

01.95   Pump Station S-133.

This is one of the many pump stations around Lake Okeechobee. It is used to pump water either into or out of the lake during times of flooding or drought.

Taylor Creek Lodge, an adult mobile home and RV park with a marina, is along the north bank of the rim canal.

02.20   Taylor Creek Lock S-193.

The Taylor Creek lock is one of the busiest in the northern sector of Lake Okeechobee, serving Taylor Creek and rim canal boaters. It is one of eight locks around Lake Okeechobee, and one of four that have to be detoured around. From the west side hikers and bikers need to proceed to the highway, cross the Taylor Creek bridge, and go back to the dike from the east side of the creek.

Note the small grove of deciduous trees on the lake side between the pump station and the lock. This is a stand of native hackberry trees, and they are a favorite roosting place for turkey vultures, black vultures, and, in the evenings, some species of waterbirds.

No fishing is allowed adjacent to the locks.

There is a great view of Lake Okeechobee and of Taylor Creek from this vantage point.

The U.S. Highway 441/State Route 98 bridge over

TAYLOR CREEK
Taylor Creek, one of the three major natural streams that flow into Lake Okeechobee, occasionally gets a visit from a manatee. There are posted signs along the creek, warning boaters to beware of these gentle creatures. Manatees, presumably not native to Lake Okeechobee, make their way in through locks. Sometimes one gets crushed in the process.

Taylor Creek is a drawbridge that allows passage of sailboats.

Fossils are abundant in the debris around the lock area.

End of Leg 1.

Leg 2: Taylor Creek to Nubbin Slough: 2.5 miles

Leg 2 is along a fairly densely populated part of the greater Okeechobee area. Vegetation on the lakeshore and the rim canal is predominantly Brazilian pepper, casuarina, and a few sabal palms. There are good views of the lake between the taller trees.

00.00   Starting point: Taylor Creek Lock.
            Proceed east along top of dike.
            Taylor Creek Condominiums are on the rim canal immediately east of the lock.
            The Treasure Island water tower can be seen on the left.
00.20   The dike curves to the southeast to an azimuth of 100 degrees.
00.30   Casuarina ends, and there is an excellent view of Lake Okeechobee.
00.40   VFW Hall 10539 is on the rim canal. Mobile homes and RV parks are along the canal.
00.50   The dike swings southeast to an azimuth of 125 degrees.

Some nice private homes are along the rim canal.

There is a good view of the rim canal, as Brazilian pepper is reduced to scattered clumps, and an excellent lake view.

01.25 Floodgate 8.

This is a little hand-operated floodgate on a small slough.

There are abundant fossils on the lakeshore near the floodgate.

A large mobile home/RV resort is across the rim canal. Live oak, cypress, and sabal palm trees are in the background.

Eagles and ospreys are sometimes seen fishing the shallow waters of the Lake Okeechobee shoreline in this area. They often rest and watch the lake from vantage points along the top of the dike.

01.70 Casuarina reappears in small stands.

Between stands of casuarina, there are excellent views of Lake Okeechobee.

There are some beautiful private homes along the rim canal.

02.10 The levee doglegs left/right before reaching Nubbin Slough (see p. 79).

02.50 Nubbin Slough Floodgates S-191.

These are large floodgates without lock access to Lake Okeechobee. The electrically-operated gates open and close to let water either into or out of Lake Okeechobee or Nubbin Slough as the need arises. They are monitored and operated by remote control from the West Palm Beach office of the South Florida Water Management District.

The northeast corner of the Nubbin Slough Floodgates is a great vantage point for a panoramic view, looking east down the rim canal, north down Nubbin Slough, and south onto Lake Okeechobee. Just past Nubbin Slough, on U.S. Route 441/State Route 98, is Upthegrove Beach, the only town directly on the north shore of the lake.

End of Leg 2.

Leg 3: Nubbin Slough to Henry Creek 3.5 miles

This is a scenic trip. Vegetation thins out with only some low-lying Brazilian pepper trees along the lakeshore, allowing great views of Lake Okeechobee along most of the way.

00.00   Starting point: Nubbin Slough Floodgates.
         Proceed southeast on top of dike.
         There are private homes on the rim canal.
00.10   The dike swings northward to an azimuth of 120 degrees.
         Beautiful homes are along the rim canal.
         The dense vegetation along the south bank of the rim canal is mostly Brazilian pepper. Also, Brazilian pepper begins to increase in clumps along the lake-front; however, since this exotic tree seldom exceeds fifteen to twenty feet in height, it does not seriously obstruct lake views from the thirty-four-foot-high levee.
01.10   The dike begins to swing to the southeast to an azimuth of 130 degrees.
         There are beautiful private homes along the rim canal and a few RV resorts and fishing camps.
01.50   Small log cabins, followed by mobile homes and RV resorts, are along the rim canal.
02.10   The dike swings southeast to an azimuth of 140 degrees.
         Dense vegetation along the rim canal continues to be dominated by Brazilian pepper. The heavy tree growth in the background across the highway is mostly cypress, live oak, and sabal palm trees.
02.60   The dike swings northeast to an azimuth of 130 degrees.

A trailer park and RV resort and many beautiful private homes are along the rim canal.

Brazilian pepper trees become denser on the lakefront.

03.50 Henry Creek Lock (G-36).

This is a small lock allowing boaters access to Lake Okeechobee from the rim canal.

Fossils are abundant in the rubble along the west bank of the lock.

This is a popular fishing spot, particularly off the small jetty that extends about 150 yards from the lock to the channel entrance off Lake Okeechobee.

There is a great view of Lake Okeechobee from the lock site.

End of Leg 3.

Leg 4: Henry Creek to Chancey Bay: 6.7 miles

This is a fairly desolate section with great views of Lake Okeechobee throughout. Both the lakeshore and the rim canal are lined with Brazilian pepper trees along much of the route.

00.00 Starting point: Henry Creek Lock.

Proceed southeast on top of dike, azimuth 130 degrees.

00.70 A small RV park is on the rim canal.

01.50 The dike swings southeast to an azimuth of 150 degrees.

01.60 RV resorts are on the rim canal for the next two tenths of a mile, with an occasional private home.

03.50 The dike begins swinging to the southeast.

03.60 The dike now trends at an azimuth of 140 degrees.

04.80 The dike begins to gradually swing southward.

A marshy area extends about a quarter mile to over

a mile from the shore into Lake Okeechobee in places along this leg. The marsh is a haven for wildlife.

05.30   The dike swings southward to an azimuth of 160 degrees.

05.50   The dike swings sharply south to an azimuth of 180 degrees (due south).

Some fossils can be seen in occasional bare spots along the sides of the dike.

06.10   The dike begins a right-left dogleg to the lock.

06.30   A Florida Trail campsite is on a flat spot along the base of the dike near the lakeshore. This campsite has a poor view due to Brazilian pepper trees.

06.40   The trail crosses an access road that extends from the highway across the rim canal to the top of the dike and to the lock.

06.70   Chancey Bay S-135 Pump Station and a small lock.
This is a beautiful spot with a great view of the lake and the nice private homes along the rim canal. Two stone jetties extend about one hundred yards out into the lake and make great fishing spots. There is little marshy land in this area. Alligators may be seen occasionally along the shore.

End of Leg 4.

Leg 5: Chancey Bay to Port Mayaca: 7.6 miles

This is a fairly desolate section with great views of Lake Okeechobee throughout most of the trip.

00.00   Starting point: Chancey Bay Lock.
Proceed southeast along dike.

01.00   The dike trends at an azimuth of 160 degrees.

01.90   Tall smokestacks in the distance to the left are part of the Martin County Power Plant. The Barley Barber Swamp, a nature preserve, is on the grounds of the plant.

02.40   A unique round house (a private home) is on the rim
canal.

03.60   The dike heading is now at an azimuth of 170 degrees.

Great lake views continue, with no marsh offshore
in this area.

Occasional private homes are along the wide rim
canal.

Port Mayaca Bridge can be seen far ahead.

05.40   The dike swings to an azimuth of 160 degrees.

Brazilian pepper trees begin to thicken along the
lakeshore, but there are still good views.

06.40   The dike swings to an azimuth of 170 degrees.

07.40   Entering Port Mayaca (see pp. 106-107).

Pavement, part of the access road, begins here on
top of the dike and continues to the Port Mayaca
Lock. The road doglegs left/right to the lock.

07.60   Port Mayaca hurricane floodgates and lock.

The wide rim canal dead-ends at this point and there
is no access from it into Lake Okeechobee.

The largest town nearby is Indiantown, about ten
miles east. There are several attractions in and near
Indiantown (see pp. 107-112).

End of Leg 5.

Leg 6: Port Mayaca to Canal Point: 9.0 miles

This leg parallels the Okeechobee Waterway, which runs just
offshore. Most of this trip is along a fairly desolate stretch
with some great views of Lake Okeechobee. The rim canal is
not navigable from this point on.

00.00   Starting point: Port Mayaca Lock.

Note: Passage across the lock is not permitted. Hikers
and bikers have to exit the dike trail on the access road
to U.S. Route 441/State Route 78 and proceed across
the high bridge over the St. Lucie Canal, then back to
the dike trail on the east side of the lock.

00.30   Continue east on the dike at an azimuth of 170 degrees.

There are no marshes near the shore in this area. Great views of Lake Okeechobee continue. The rim canal is abandoned and overgrown with brush and trees.

01.40   The dike swings to an azimuth of 175 degrees.

01.45   Floodgate.

This floodgate is for a small canal that leads into the lake. The canal drains cane fields to the northeast.

Red and green triangular channel signs in the lake near the shore mark the Okeechobee Waterway. Boaters have a choice of following either the waterway which runs adjacent to the shore all the way from Port Mayaca to Moore Haven (Route 2) or taking the shorter way by cutting directly across Lake Okee-chobee (Route 1).

01.70   The dike turns to an azimuth of 180 degrees (due south).

02.40   Floodgate 16.

This small floodgate connects a drainage canal into Lake Okeechobee. The jetties leading away from the floodgate and into the lake are good fishing spots.

The rim canal remains abandoned from here to the west side of Lake Okeechobee, except for a short section at Clewiston.

There are continued great views of Lake Okeechobee.

Vast cane fields can be seen in the distance to the left.

02.70   The dike swings to an azimuth of 190 degrees.

02.90   A Florida Trail campsite is on a flat spot at the base of the dike. This site has a fairly good view of the lake and the Okeechobee Waterway. This is also a great campsite for viewing sunsets.

03.00   Power lines enter from the north and head south

along the dike. A small drainage canal enters the abandoned rim canal at this point.

04.20 Floodgate 14.

This floodgate connects a small drainage canal from the cane fields into Lake Okeechobee.

Great views of Lake Okeechobee continue and there is a good view of Port Mayaca Bridge to the rear. The town of Pahokee and Kramer Island can be seen in the far distance. Railroad tracks now parallel the abandoned rim canal. Vast cane fields are seen to the left.

04.70 The dike swings to an azimuth of 180 (due south).

04.90 Floodgate 10A.

This floodgate is on a large canal that drains cane fields in the north into Lake Okeechobee. The canal is diked to about ten feet high on either side, which allows it to cut across the abandoned rim canal. There are good views of cane fields to east and Lake Okeechobee to west. This is a popular fishing spot. Fossils are abundant in the rubble around the floodgate.

05.20 The dike curves to an azimuth of 170 degrees. There is a great view of cane fields and a big sugar mill in the distance. A large stand of banana trees is on the far side of the rim canal, which is now just a narrow, abandoned ditch. Great views of Lake Okeechobee continue.

05.90 The dike begins a long, sweeping curve to the southwest toward Pahokee.

06.10 Floodgate 13.

This floodgate is on a small canal that drains the cane fields. The jetties leading to the gate are good fishing spots. There are abundant fossils in the rubble. The dike continues a broad swing to the southeast.

06.80 The dike straightens to an azimuth of 205 degrees. The railroad tracks, power lines, and the Okeechobee

Waterway, offshore, all continue to parallel the dike. Great lake views continue.

07.20 The dike swings to an azimuth of 210 degrees.

08.30 At this point, the trail is entering the Canal Point area. Trailers and houses begin to appear across the highway. The dike now trends at an azimuth of 220 degrees.

08.40 Tall casuarina trees begin to partially block the lake view.

08.50 The building across the street is a sugarcane field station of the U.S. Department of Agriculture.

08.80 The Canal Point water tower is to the left.

08.90 The dike trail crosses the access road to Canal Point Town Park.

Hikers and bikers can easily exit the dike here for a tour through the small community of Canal Point (see pp. 112-113).

09.00 West Palm Beach Canal and Floodgates S-352 (no lock).

The area around the floodgates and the highway bridge over the canal are popular fishing spots.

The Connors Highway parallels the south side of the West Palm Beach Canal as it extends east toward West Palm Beach.

End of Leg 6.

Leg 7: Canal Point to Pahokee: 3.6 miles

This leg parallels a populated sector of Pahokee. The beautiful royal palm trees that line many of Pahokee's streets can be seen. The Okeechobee Waterway continues offshore. Lake views are limited due to tall casuarina trees.

00.00 Starting point: West Palm Beach Canal.

Proceed southwest on the trail toward Pahokee, azimuth 210 degrees.

00.20   U.S. Sugar's huge Bryant Mill can be seen to the east. There are seven sugar mills in the Everglades. Besides the Bryant Mill, they are: U.S. Sugar's Clewiston Mill, Osceola Farms Company Mill, Okeelanta Mill, Talisman Sugar Corporation Mill, Atlantic Sugar Association Mill, and the Sugar Cane Growers of Florida Mill.

00.40   There is a good view of Lake Okeechobee at a large gap in the casuarina trees.

00.50   Jones Fish House is to the left (see p. 113).

01.00   There is a good scenic view of the lake here through a gap in the casuarina trees.

01.30   Gaps in casuarina trees allow some lake views.

There is a road across the highway leads to the sugar mill, seen clearly in the distance.

Vast cane fields are across the highway.

01.50   The dike swings to an azimuth of 200 degrees.

01.70   Beautiful royal palms can be seen lining the highway.

01.80   The Pahokee water tower is on the left.

02.00   The dike now heads at an azimuth of 210 degrees.

There are great views of the lake through gaps in the casuarina.

Royal palms can be seen lining the streets of Pahokee

02.20   A big steel tower is across the highway.

There is a good lake view here through a gap in the trees.

02.10   The dike now trends at an azimuth of 220 degrees.

03.00   The dike swings slightly right as the Pahokee Marina & Campground is approached (see p. 104).

03.60   The trail intersects the access road to the Pahokee Marina & Campground.

The Pahokee Chamber of Commerce is just a block east.

Bikers and hikers can sometimes dine at a boat tied

up at the marina. Pam's Seafood Restaurant and Market, just two blocks east, is highly recommended for fresh Lake Okeechobee catfish

The Pahokee Marina & Campground is one of the best places on the lake to view a sunset. Public restrooms are available here.

End of Leg 7.

Leg 8: Pahokee to Paul Rardin Park: 6.3 miles

This leg is characterized by generally great views of Lake Okeechobee and the vast cane fields. The Okeechobee Waterway continues to parallel the dike and is just offshore. Watch for southern Florida's unique bird, the smooth-billed ani, commonly seen along the more southern shores of the lake.

00.00   Starting point: Pahokee Marina & Campground.
        Proceed southwest on the paved dike trail, azimuth 250 degrees.
00.10   Campgrounds are on the right, at the edge of the lake.
        The trees along the shore are Australian pine (casuarina). There are good views of the lake between gaps in the trees. These trees make good windbreaks and were planted here for that purpose.
        Royal palms can be seen lining Pahokee's streets to the left.
00.60   The end of the campground, and the end of the pavement.
01.60   The dike begins to swing to the left to an azimuth of 230 degrees.
        The trees along the lake have now thinned out and the lake view is good. Only scattered Brazilian pepper trees remain.
        Kramer Island can be seen clearly in the distance.
02.00   Vast cane fields can be seen across highway to left.

    Many royal palms are visible to the left.

02.40   The dike swings sharply left to an azimuth of 180 degrees (due south).

02.60   There are continued good views of the royal palm trees of Pahokee to the left.

02.80   A small canal that drains the cane fields to the east goes into Lake Okeechobee.

    This marks the approximate southern limit of the beautiful royal palm trees that line many of Pahokee's streets.

    From this point and for another mile southward, there are very abundant fossil shells along the lakeshore.

02.90   The dike swings slightly to the southwest, to an azimuth of 190 degrees.

03.40   The Glades County Airport is on the left.

    There is little vegetation on either side of the dike and the view is great. On the right is the Okeechobee Waterway, and beyond is Kramer Island. On the left, past the airport, are huge cane fields. A large sugar refinery can be seen in the distance.

03.90   The dike curves to the left to an azimuth of 160 degrees.

    There is a great view off to both sides of the dike from here.

    Kramer Island is due west of this point, about two miles offshore.

    The Okeechobee Waterway is now a dredged canal that parallels the shore. The canal continues in this form from here to Moore Haven. Debris from the dredging forms a tree-covered linear mound on the lake side of the waterway.

04.30   A small canal that drains the cane fields enters Lake Okeechobee.

    This area has been used an access point for launching boats, but it is an unofficial one and the launch site is primitive.

Trees, mainly casuarina, have gradually increased and are becoming dense along the foot of the dike at the lakefront. The view of the lake is restricted by these trees, but a good view of the cane fields continues.

05.20 The dike takes a slight dogleg to the left/right, returning to its original course.

Dense, tall casuarina trees begin along the foot of the dike on the lakefront. These casuarina, and the trees (mostly casuarina) on the bank on the other side of the waterway, block most of the lake view. Good views, however, remain to the left.

05.40 A wide, marshy southern coastline of Lake Okeechobee begins developing in this area, as seen through gaps in the trees.

The highway, Becom Road (County Route 715), runs adjacent to the dike. There is no rim canal, just a very small drainage ditch.

06.00 The dike begins curving to the right (southwestward).

06.30 Paul Rardin Park.

End of Leg 8.

Leg 9: Paul Rardin Park to Belle Glade Marina Campground: 3.6 miles

The lake side along the dike and the mound on the lake side of the Okeechobee Waterway are lined with casuarina trees for most of this leg, obstructing the view, although there are good views of the cane fields to the left. Beehives begin appearing along the sides of the dike, and are seen in many places along the dike from here to the northwest side of the lake.

00.00 Starting point: Paul Rardin Park.
Proceed southwest on the dike, azimuth 230 degrees.

00.10 Good view of the marshy south side of Lake

PAUL RARDIN PARK
This small park has picnic facilities and restrooms. The road into the park is lined with royal palm trees. Oak trees in the park are threatened by the Florida strangler fig, which can kill its host tree.

Okeechobee and the islands at a gap in the casuarina trees.

A huge sugar refinery can be seen to the left.

A large rim canal is present from this point for the next six-tenths mile. This appears to be a failed development project.

Occasional stands of melaleuca are now seen along the far bank of the Okeechobee Waterway.

00.70   This marks the end of the rim canal.

00.90   Occasional melaleuca trees now appear on the dike side of the lake, with denser stands on the far bank of the waterway. Casuarina is so dense that one can hardly see the adjacent Okeechobee Waterway.

01.70   There is a continuing great view of the cane fields.

02.00   Floodgate.

This floodgate, on a small drainage canal that drains into Lake Okeechobee, has a service road that extends over the dike to the gate. However, this is not a public access point.

The dike swings sharply left to an azimuth of 200 degrees.

03.30   The dike curves right to an azimuth of 210 degrees.

There is a good view of the marshy south side of Lake Okeechobee through gaps in the casuarina.

Good views of the cane fields continue, and a sugar refinery can be seen in the distance.

It is interesting to note that the cane fields are separated into large tracts, each at a different stage of growth. Some plots may have cane more than twelve feet tall with many brown leaves, particularly in fall or winter. The brown leaves usually indicate that the cane is mature and ready to burn and harvest. Other fields may be in the process of being plowed and planted. The planting of sugarcane involves laying cuttings of cane stalks in furrows and covering them with muck. At each joint of the buried stalk, several shoots of new cane growth will appear, forming a cluster of sugarcane. It takes about twelve to fifteen months for the cane to reach maturity and be ready for harvesting.

03.60   The dike intersects the paved road that leads to the right over a swing bridge to the Belle Glade Marina Campground on Torry Island (see pp. 100-101).

The Belle Glade Municipal Golf Course is to the left, and the Drawbridge Cafe is a short distance up the road to the left

End of Leg 9.

Leg 10: Belle Glade Marina Campground to South Bay Campground: 2.0 miles

This leg continues along an area where thick casuarina and melaleuca trees line the lake side of the dike and the far side of the Okeechobee Waterway.

00.00   Starting point: The access road to the Belle Glade Marina Campground.

Proceed southwest on dike trail at an azimuth of 210 degrees.

00.30   Hillsboro Canal, hurricane floodgates, and pump station (no lock).

The Hillsboro Canal is one of the largest canals connected to Lake Okeechobee. The canal waterway is divided into one channel for the floodgates and one for the pumps.

00.70 Torry Island can be seen offshore in Lake Okeechobee, across the Okeechobee Waterway. This point is the approximate southwest end of the island.

Some open water of Lake Okeechobee, along with marshlands, can be seen between gaps in the trees.

01.80 A dredged pile of limestone debris on the lake side of the dike here is loaded with fossil shells.

02.00 South Bay Campground.

At this point the dike trail intersects the road that leads over the dike to the boat ramps for the South Bay Campground.

There is a good view of Lake Okeechobee here. Marshlands and open water can be seen in the distance.

South Bay Campground, with restroom facilities, is on the left.

End of Leg 10.

Leg 11: South Bay Campground to John Stretch Park: 5.2 miles

This trip offers occasional good views of Lake Okeechobee, but along much of the way the view is blocked by dense stands of casuarina and melaleuca trees.

00.00 Starting point: South Bay Campground.

Proceed southwestward along the dike.

The dike begins a long swing to the right (west ward).

00.20 The dike has now straightened to an azimuth of 280 degrees.

The highway, U.S. Route 27, is now adjacent to the dike.

Vast cane fields can be seen on the other side of the highway.

There is a good view of Lake Okeechobee at this point.

00.50 Dense growth of casuarina trees nearly blocks out the view of the lake.

Melaleuca is the predominant tree on the far side of the Okeechobee Waterway. In time, if the melaleuca is not controlled, it will probably form a monoculture and crowd out everything else.

00.70 The dike begins a slight dogleg left/right and then goes back to its original course at an azimuth of 280 degrees.

01.30 Floodgate.

A small cane field drainage canal leads into the lake here.

01.40 The dike swings to the right to an azimuth of 310 degrees.

02.20 Lake Okeechobee can be seen in places where there are gaps in the trees.

The lake has open water in this area.

02.90 The dike begins a very gentle swing to the left.

03.70 The swing is now complete and the dike trends at an azimuth of 270 degrees (due west).

Melaleuca increases in this area.

Large cane fields can be seen across the highway.

04.30 There are occasional gaps in the trees where the open water and marshes of Lake Okeechobee can be seen.

04.50 The highway veers to the left and away from the dike.

04.90 The lake view is largely blocked by casuarina trees and the view to the left is blocked by live oak trees and other vegetation.

05.20 Miami Canal floodgates and pump station (no lock) and John Stretch Park.

The Miami Canal is one of the largest canals connected to Lake Okeechobee. It is divided into two channels, one for the pump station and one for the floodgates.

A large limestone debris pile on the east side of the canal has abundant fossils. Exotic granite riprap has been placed around the banks of the canal.

The entrance to John Stretch Park is off the highway on the west side of the canal. There are picnic tables and restrooms in the park.

End of Leg 11.

Leg 12: John Stretch Park to Clewiston: 8.4 miles

This section of the trail is characterized by continuing dense stands of casuarina and melaleuca trees along the lake side of the dike and on the far side of the Okeechobee Waterway, which parallels the shore. Lake views are limited to a few places where there are gaps in the trees.

00.00   Starting point: John Stretch Park, on the east side of the Miami Canal.

Proceed west on the trail, azimuth 270 degrees (due west).

00.30   John Stretch Park ends here.

The highway, U.S. Route 27, is about four hundred yards from the trail.

00.50   A small lake is adjacent to the dike. Its water is brown due to tannic acid from the abundant vegetation around the lake. Lake Okeechobee, as well as many of southern Florida's streams and lakes, has a similar brown color from tannic acid.

Brazilian pepper trees begin to line the left side of the dike, while casuarina continues to line the lake side.

00.70   The dike begins a long swing to the right.

01.00   The dike straightens to an azimuth of 320 degrees.

The highway is now adjacent to the dike, with good views across it to the cane fields.

01.40   A Florida National Scenic Trail campsite (#22) is on a flat spot along the base of the dike on the lake side. The lake view is obstructed by casuarina trees.

03.10   A gap in the trees allows a glimpse of Lake Okeechobee. There is not as much marshland in this area; it is mostly open water.

     A large sugar refinery can be seen in the distance.

03.30   The dike begins to curve to the left.

03.70   Floodgate and Pump Station S-236.

     This floodgate and pump station are on a small canal that drains sugarcane fields. The canal is divided into two channels here, one for the floodgate and one for the pump station.

     There is a great view of open water of Lake Okeechobee from here. The dike has now straightened to an azimuth of 320 degrees.

04.20   Dense melaleuca now lines the far side of the Okeechobee Waterway. Casuarina remains the dominant vegetation on the lake side of the dike.

     Some cattle pasturage is now present to the left, but most of the fields are still sugarcane.

05.20   The dike curves to the left to an azimuth of 310 degrees.

05.50   The Crooked Hook RV resort is across the highway.

06.30   A large stand of young melaleuca trees begins to appear on the far side of the highway, blocking views of the cane fields.

06.40   A plant-choked rim canal, about thirty feet wide, now runs adjacent to the dike. Brazilian pepper trees line the canal's far bank. This creates a small wildlife refuge right next to the highway.

07.30   The dike swings to the right to an azimuth of 320 degrees.

07.50   Pump station.

     This is a small electric pump with no floodgates.

     Casuarina trees continue on the lake side of the dike

and melaleuca trees on the far side of the waterway. The line of melaleuca trees continues to parallel the far side of the highway. The abandoned rim canal continues.

07.80   There is a good view of Lake Okeechobee through a gap in the trees.

08.30   This point marks the end of the rim canal and the termination of the long line of melaleuca trees across the highway.

08.40   Clewiston (see pp. 93-95).

Canal and lock.

This waterway, the Industrial Canal, and the lock allow boaters in Clewiston to enter Lake Okeechobee.

There is a good view of Lake Okeechobee from here.

Hikers and bikers are not able to pass over the canal. To get to the other side, take the road to the left (south), which leads past the South Florida Operation Office of the U.S. Army Corps of Engineers, about a half-mile to the highway. Take the highway west over the canal, turn right on Esperanza Avenue, then right again on North Francisco Street. Proceed about three-tenths mile and turn left toward the Clewiston boat ramps and the top of the dike.

End of Leg 12.

Leg 13: Clewiston to Moore Haven: 12.6 miles

This leg, the longest of the tour, could be divided into two parts, using Uncle Joe's Fish Camp, five and six-tenths miles from Clewiston, as an access point. However, since the fish camp is private property, the leg is from Clewiston to Moore Haven, spanning two public access areas. This route continues to have dense casuarina and melaleuca trees that block the view of Lake Okeechobee along much of the way.

00.00   Starting point: The west side of the Industrial Canal at Clewiston.

Proceed northwest along the dike trail, azimuth 320 degrees.

A large rim canal parallels the dike in this area.

00.10   The Herbert Hoover Memorial Park, with boat ramps and several picnic tables, is adjacent to the dike, on the Lake Okeechobee shore. The Okeechobee Waterway is just offshore.

00.20   Boat ramps and a large parking lot are on the left side, across the rim canal. Boats launched here must pass through the Clewiston Lock to reach Lake Okeechobee.

00.50   This point marks the northwest end of the Herbert Hoover Memorial Park.

00.60   There is a good view of Lake Okeechobee here. There are no casuarina trees along the dike in this area. The far bank of the waterway, however, has a mixture of casuarina and melaleuca trees.

00.80   The dike curves to the right to an azimuth of 325 degrees.

The main canal now veers to the left and away from the dike. A small, unused, and overgrown rim canal continues along the side of the dike. The view to the left is restricted by a mixture of trees and shrubs, but there is a great view down the Okeechobee Waterway.

01.10   There is a good view of Lake Okeechobee from here, between stands of melaleuca on the far side of the waterway. Extensive shallow marshes occur in this area, but open water can be seen beyond the marshland.

Melaleuca trees begin to appear to the left, across the rim canal. The small, weed-choked canal provides a good wildlife refuge. It should be a good fishing hole since is remotely located, away from more accessible water.

The highway no longer runs adjacent to the dike.

02.70   The rim canal is now largely grown over with vegetation.

03.40   Pump Station S-4.

This pump station is on a large canal that is connected to Lake Okeechobee.

The melaleuca and other trees that blocked the view to the left are now gone and cane fields can be seen again. There is little vegetation on either side of the dike here, but melaleuca continues to grow on the far side of the waterway.

A large and clear rim canal now parallels the dike.

03.80   The marshy southern side of Lake Okeechobee can be seen to the right.

03.90   The dike curves to the northwest, to an azimuth of 330 degrees.

Vast cane fields are seen to the left.

04.40   The melaleuca trees on the far side of the waterway end, and there is a good view of the marshes of southern Lake Okeechobee.

A line of melaleuca that extends out into the marshes marks a boat channel. This channel is part of the alternate route (Route 1A) of the Okeechobee Waterway that boaters can take across the lake from Port Mayaca to Moore Haven.

05.60   The dike trail intersects a road over the dike that leads to a private boat ramp and dock for Uncle Joe's Fish Camp.

Uncle Joe's Fish Camp is to the left. The base of the dike was widened here for the camp, and the rim canal was diverted around the site.

The dike begins to swing to the left.

05.70   The dike has now straightened to an azimuth of 270 degrees (due west).

This site offers a panoramic view of the lake on the right and cane fields on the left. The dike is relatively free of vegetation in this area.

06.00   The dike begins to turn toward the right.

06.10   The dike straightens to an azimuth of 280 degrees.

06.90   The dike turns northwest to an azimuth of 290 degrees.

07.20   Floodgates.

These floodgates are on a small canal that is connected to the lake.

The rim canal continues along the dike.

Swinging sharply left, the dike now heads at an azimuth of 230 degrees.

Casuarina reappears on the lake side of the dike, obstructing the view, but good views of the cane fields continue on the left.

08.20   The dike begins to swing to the northwest.

Casuarina continues on the lake side of the dike, mixed with some Brazilian pepper trees. Dense melaleuca are now seen on the far side of the Okeechobee Waterway.

08.30   The dike straightens to an azimuth of 275 degrees.

09.50   The dike turns slightly left to an azimuth of 270 degrees (due west).

09.80   Sabal palms begin to appear along the rim canal.

A water tower is to the left.

09.90   A Florida National Scenic Trail campsite (#3) is along the base of the dike, adjacent to the rim canal.

10.30   The dike begins a gentle swing to the right.

10.70   The dike has now straightened to an azimuth of 350 degrees.

10.90   Canal.

This is a small drainage canal connected to Lake Okeechobee.

11.00   Melaleuca trees begin to appear on the lake side of the dike.

Large cane fields are seen to the left.

11.60   The dike swings westward to an azimuth of 290 degrees.

11.80   At this point, the Okeechobee Waterway deviates from the side of the dike and lies about three hundred yards to the north. Its site is marked by a line of melaleuca on its far bank. Several sabal palms are seen in the field between the dike and the waterway. A line of melaleuca also extends along the outer bank of the rim canal.

12.20   The Alvin L. Ward Sr. Memorial Park, with boat ramps and picnic tables, is to the right.

12.50   Floodgates.

These floodgates are for the Caloosahatchee River.

The banks of the river, adjacent to the floodgates, are popular fishing spots.

12.50   Moore Haven Lock on the Caloosahatchee River.

Hikers and bikers must detour around the lock. To get to the other side, take the road to the left about a half-mile to the highway, turn right, and cross the bridge over the Caloosahatchee River. After crossing the bridge, turn right on 1st Street and proceed back to the dike.

Moore Haven (see pp. 115-117). Food, refreshments, and restroom facilities can be found in town.

End of Leg 13.

Leg 14: Moore Haven to Sportsman's Village Park: 7.0 miles

Leg 14 is along the marshy southwest side of Lake Okeechobee. Beef cattle pasturage is seen on the left along the dike. The dominant vegetation along the route is Brazilian pepper, melaleuca, and sabal palm trees.

00.00   Starting point: West side of the Moore Haven Lock on the Caloosahatchee River.

Note: This requires some maneuvering if one starts at the lock because a fence separates Sportsman's Marina and Campground from the lock area.

Proceed northwest on the dike, azimuth 325 degrees.

00.10   Sportsman's Marina and Campground.

This marina and campground, operated by A Thousand Adventures, Inc., on land leased from the U.S. Army Corps of Engineers, is within the dike, directly on the shore of Lake Okeechobee.

A small clogged-up rim canal is adjacent to the dike, with melaleuca lining its far bank.

00.40   Abundant, scattered sabal palm trees are now appearing in the areas off both sides of the dike. The lake does not approach the dike here (the Okeechobee Waterway ended at Moore Haven).

00.60   Melaleuca trees are becoming thicker on the lake side of the dike, completely blocking the view in places, and they continue along the far side of the rim canal.

Large beef cattle pasturage can be seen to the left.

01.00   The melaleuca ends on the lake side of the dike and there is a good view of the marshy west side of Lake Okeechobee. Some melaleuca and abundant Brazilian pepper are growing on the banks of the rim canal.

01.70   A long line of melaleuca can be seen extending along the lake, about three-quarters mile from the dike.

Dense Brazilian pepper trees are along the rim canal.

03.00   There is a good view of beef cattle pasturage to the left. Sabal palms are scattered throughout the fields.

Wide marshlands with dense scrub vegetation are on the lake side to the right.

The highway, State Route 78, can be seen in the distance to the left.

03.40   The dike begins a very slight dogleg left/right.

03.70   The dike begins to swing to the right.

03.90   Floodgates.

These floodgates are for a small canal which drains cane fields and pasturage to the west and connects into Lake Okeechobee.

The highway is now adjacent to the dike, across the vegetation-clogged rim canal.

Dense Brazilian pepper trees across the highway obstruct the view past the road.

The view to the lake side of the dike is across a wide expanse of marshland. The line of melaleuca trees in the distance ends at this point.

The dike has straightened to an azimuth of 10 degrees.

04.40   Tall stands of melaleuca now reappear along the lake side. Brazilian pepper continues to be the dominant vegetation along the highway and the rim canal.

04.60   The large hill seen across the highway is an old Moore Haven landfill.

Large cane fields can be seen to the left, across the highway.

05.00   The melaleuca trees are becoming dense on the lake side of the dike. Brazilian pepper is now absent from the road side, and there is a good view of the cane fields from here. However, these trees continue to be thick along the rim canal.

Sandhill cranes, ospreys, and caracaras are often observed in this area.

05.40   The cane fields have now been largely replaced by cattle pasture.

06.30   Floodgates C-5.

These floodgates are for Nicodemus Slough, a large canal that drains the cane fields and pastures to the west and connects to Lake Okeechobee. There is a good view of the marshy wetlands of the western side of Lake Okeechobee from here. There is also a good view of the pasture land to the left, across the highway.

06.50   There is a good view from here of the marshlands and a large, dredged channel that extends from the shore ahead and out into the lake.

06.60 The dike begins to swing to the left, where it extends across the highway and continues to the northwest.

06.70 Highway.

State Route 78 goes over the dike and continues on the lake side of the dike for about three miles. This is the only area around Lake Okeechobee where the highway is between the dike and the lake for any appreciable distance. It does the same thing, but for only a short distance, on the east side of the Kissimmee River.

Proceed northward along the highway, azimuth 30 degrees.

06.90 The highway crosses a bridge over a large slough at this point.

07.00 Sportsman's Village.

This small park on the right has a parking lot, boat ramps, and a picnic area. Boats are launched into the adjoining slough and can proceed down the channel to the open waters of Lake Okeechobee.

End of Leg 14.

Leg 15: Sportsman's Village to Lakeport: 2.8 miles

This entire leg traverses the highway, State Route 78. Dense growths of Brazilian pepper trees obstruct views on both sides of the highway along much of the route.

00.00 Starting point: Sportsman's Village.

Proceed northward on the highway, azimuth 30 degrees.

01.60 The unimproved road to the right leads to the Vance W. Whidden Recreation Area and Curry Island. A permit is needed to enter because it has been the site of illegal dumping in the past. Curry Island is a high sand ridge that parallels the shore of Lake Okeechobee. It is surrounded by marshlands.

01.80   Bridge.

The highway crosses over a small slough at this point.

02.00   The highway begins to curve to the right.

02.40   Fisheating Creek.

There is a good view of the marshlands of the lake from the bridge.

Proceed ahead on the highway, azimuth 40 degrees.

02.80   Entering Lakeport (see pp. 119-121).

The highway crosses over a slough. On the far side of the bridge there is a small park with a boat ramp and picnic tables.

End of Leg 15.

Leg 16: Lakeport to Margaret Van de Velde Park: 4.3 miles

On this leg, the dike parallels a populated sector of Lakeport waterfront along a wide rim canal. Views of Lake Okeechobee are limited by dense growths of melaleuca trees.

00.00   Starting point: On State Route 78, at the south line of Lakeport, adjacent to the small park just north of Fisheating Creek.

Proceed northeast on the highway, azimuth 40 degrees.

00.10   Herbert Hoover Dike.

The highway intersects and goes over the dike. From here to Okeechobee, the dike will be between the highway and the marshlands of western Lake Okeechobee.

Turn right and proceed along the dike, azimuth 70 degrees. Here the view toward the lake is entirely blocked by melaleuca trees.

00.30   The dike begins to curve to the left, to an azimuth of 50 degrees. A large trailer park can be seen across the highway. A big rim canal borders the west side of the dike, much of its banks lined with Brazilian pepper trees.

00.80 The dike begins to swing to the right.

Hundreds of sabal palm trees can be seen in the fields to the left.

01.00 The dike has straightened to an azimuth of 90 degrees (due east).

02.00 Small lock and Pump Station S-131.

There is a good view of the marshy west side of Lake Okeechobee from here through a gap in the melaleuca trees. Private homes are seen across the rim canal.

02.10 The dike begins a long swing to the left. Dense melaleuca again block the lake view. Several Lakeport homes can be seen across the rim canal.

02.50 The dike straightens to an azimuth of 40 degrees.

Many beautiful homes are across the rim canal.

03.60 The dike begins to swing to the right.

03.70 The dike straightens to an azimuth of 60 degrees.

03.90 The dike swings sharply northwest to an azimuth of 340 degrees, paralleling the Harney Point Canal.

04.10 State Route 78.

The dike intersects the highway.

Turn right and proceed northeast on the highway, azimuth 50 degrees, across the bridge over the Harney Point Canal.

04.20 Herbert Hoover Dike.

Here the highway meets the dike again.

Lakeport.

A number of buildings in Lakeport lie just ahead along the highway. Included are Glenn Hunter's Guide Service, the Duck Pub, and the Lakeport Inn. Food, refreshments, and restroom facilities are available.

Turn right onto the dike and proceed southeastward, azimuth 160 degrees.

04.30   At this point, the dike turns sharply left. The entrance
        to Margaret Van de Velde Park (see p. 120) is straight
        ahead.

> End of Leg 16.

Leg 17: Margaret Van de Velde Park to Bare Beach: 1.0 mile

This leg, the shortest one of the tour, parallels a populated section of Lakeport, with many lovely homes situated along the rim canal.

00.00   Starting point: Margaret Van de Velde Park.
        Proceed northward on the dike, azimuth 60 degrees.
        The rim canal, which dead-ends at the Harney Pond
        Canal, begins again and runs parallel to the dike.
00.20   The dike swings to the left to an azimuth of 50
        degrees.
        Melaleuca trees continue along the lake side of the
        dike, along with abundant Brazilian pepper trees.
        Brazilian pepper trees and sabal palm trees are along
        the banks of the rim canal.
00.80   The dike swings slightly to the right, to an azimuth of
        60 degrees.
01.00   The dike intersects the road to Bare Beach (Dyess
        Road).
        Bare Beach is seen to the immediate right, and
        several beautiful homes to the left are across the rim
        canal. The Dyess Road causeway to Bare Beach, across
        the rim canal, divides the rim canal, prohibiting boats
        from freely traveling along its course.

> End of Leg 17.

Leg 18: Bare Beach to Indian Prairie Canal: 7.2 miles

This is a fairly desolate stretch. The rim canal continues, but there are only a few houses along its bank. The lake side of the dike is lined with melaleuca trees, obstructing views of Lake Okeechobee.

00.00   Starting point: Bare Beach.
        Proceed northward on the dike, azimuth 60 degrees.
        The banks of the rim canal are lined with Brazilian pepper trees, sabal palms, and other vegetation. Melaleuca trees line the lake side of the dike.

00.50   The dike begins to swing slightly to the right, to an azimuth of 65 degrees.
        A few waterfront homes are seen along the rim canal from this point to about three-tenths of a mile northeast of here.

01.20   A Florida National Scenic Trail campsite (#6) is along the base of the dike, on the rim canal side.
        The dike begins a slight swing to the left.

01.30   The dike straightens to an azimuth of 60 degrees.

01.70   The dike begins to curve to the right.

01.90   The dike has straightened at an azimuth of 70 degrees.

02.50   The dike begins to swing to the left.
        This is a very desolate area. Cattle pasturage can be seen across the canal, with abundant sabal palm trees scattered throughout the fields. Melaleuca continues to line the lake side.

02.90   The dike straightens at an azimuth of 40 degrees.
        A tiny community of homes is on the waterfront, on the far bank of the rim canal.

03.70   The dike begins to swing to the right, azimuth 50 degrees.

03.80   Pump Station S-129.
        At this point a small canal connects to Lake Okeechobee. The view of the lake remains limited because of melaleuca trees.

04.50   The dike begins to curve to the left.

04.80   The dike straightens to an azimuth of 30 degrees.

The highway is about a half-mile west of the dike, as marked by the utility wires.

05.50   The dike begins to swing to the right to an azimuth of 40 degrees.

06.40   The dike swings to the left to an azimuth of 30 degrees.

06.70   The dike swings sharply to the northwest to an azimuth of 330 degrees as it follows the Indian Prairie Canal.

07.20   Highway and Indian Prairie Canal.

Here the dike crosses the highway, State Route 78, and continues westward, along the southern bank of the Indian Prairie Canal.

Turn right and follow the highway, azimuth 45 degrees, to the center of the bridge over the Indian Prairie Canal. This vantage point has a great view down the canal toward Lake Okeechobee, and in the opposite direction, of the cattle range.

The Indian Prairie Campground is along the south bank of the canal, a half-mile from the highway, in the direction of Lake Okeechobee.

End of Leg 18.

Leg 19: Indian Prairie Canal to the Kissimmee River: 9.5 miles

This route leads about seven miles through a desolate countryside before reaching the small community of Buckhead Ridge, then two and a half more miles to the Kissimmee River.

00.00   Starting point: Center of the bridge over the Indian Prairie Canal.

Proceed north across the bridge, azimuth 45 degrees.

Turn right immediately after crossing the bridge and proceed on the dike, azimuth 150 degrees.

A rim canal, densely bordered with Brazilian pepper trees, follows on the left side of the dike.

00.50   The dike swings left to an azimuth of 40 degrees.

This point marks the beginning of a long line of dead melaleuca trees, killed by herbicides a few years ago in an experimental eradication program; consequently, there are good views of the marshlands of western Lake Okeechobee along this route.

01.60   Good views of Lake Okeechobee marshlands continue. The rim canal continues, with Brazilian pepper trees and sabal palms along its banks.

02.20   There is a great view of the range land to the west.

04.20   The highway now lies about two miles west of the dike. Great views continue throughout this sector.

04.70   A few ranch houses can be seen in the distance to the left, but the area remains desolate.

The Buckhead Ridge water tower can be seen in the distance ahead.

06.50   The dike begins a sharp swing to the right, after completing one of its longest straight stretches around the lake (six miles).

Houses of Buckhead Ridge can be seen ahead.

06.60   The dike straightens at an azimuth of 80 degrees.

07.00   Buckhead Ridge Lock and Pump Station S-127.

This small lock provides access to Lake Okeechobee for residents and visitors to Buckhead Ridge. The town lies to the left, across the rim canal. The Buckhead Ridge Marina and Restaurant are directly across the canal. To reach the restaurant, which is open from 6 A.M. to 2 P.M. only, take the access road from the lock to the highway, County Route 78B. Turn right and proceed one-tenth mile to the restaurant.

The Buckhead Ridge Lock also marks the end of the dead melaleuca trees. Riprap around the lock is an exotic gray granite. Some fossils from the bedrock can be seen in places below the lock.

An abandoned, weed-choked canal on the lake side of the dike begins here and extends for over a mile to the northwest, running parallel and adjacent to the dike. This canal teems with birds and other wildlife. The far side of the canal is lined with melaleuca trees.

Continue northeast on the dike, azimuth 80 degrees.

07.40   The dike begins to curve to the left.

Some beautiful homes are along the rim canal in this area.

07.50   The dike straightens to an azimuth of 25 degrees.

08.20   The dike swings to the east, to an azimuth of 40 degrees.

08.60   The abandoned canal on the lake side ends as does the line of melaleuca trees on its far bank. Also, the rim canal begins to narrow here. There is a good view of Lake Okeechobee marshlands.

08.80   The dirt road to the right leads to a Florida National Scenic Trail campsite along the road side. The road extends nearly a mile out into the marshlands, along a narrow, artificial causeway. There are primitive boat ramps along and at the end of the road where light boats and possibly air boats can be launched. The end of the causeway provides some great views of Lake Okeechobee. This makes a nice nature trail hike.

09.10   The dike swings abruptly to the west, to an azimuth of 340 degrees, to parallel the Kissimmee River. There is a great view from here of Lake Okeechobee, the Kissimmee River, and the Okee-Tantie Recreation Area on the north shore of the river.

09.40   Highway.

At this point, the dike intersects State Route 78.

Turn right and proceed over the Kissimmee River Bridge, azimuth 70 degrees.

09.50   Center of the Kissimmee River Bridge.

The dike continues to extend to the northwest, paralleling the banks of the Kissimmee River. The river is actually a deep, wide canal called "C-38." There is an excellent view to the right down the river and into Lake Okeechobee, about a mile downstream. There is also a good view of the cattle country in the upstream direction.

End of Leg 19.

Leg 20: Kissimmee River to Jaycee Park, Okeechobee: 4.3 miles

This final leg of the trip starts by following the highway a short distance inside the Herbert Hoover Dike, then back onto the dike, following it through a fairly well-populated section of the greater Okeechobee area to Jaycee Park.

00.00   Starting point: Center of the bridge over the Kissimmee River on State Route 78.

       Proceed northeast on the highway.

00.15   Swampland Tours is on the left; Okee-Tantie Recreation Area (see pp. 85-86) is on the right.

SWAMPLAND TOURS

At Swampland Tours visitors take a two-hour guided boat ride through the Audubon Reserve, where they can see a great variety of birds and other wildlife typically found in the marshlands along the western shore of Lake Okeechobee.

00.30   Mr. G's RV Resort is on the right. This is one of the few private properties inside the Hoover Dike.

00.45   Herbert Hoover Dike.

       At this point, the highway goes over the Hoover Dike. The dike trends west along the north bank of the Kissimmee River. The trail to the left, along the top of the dike, is part of the Florida National Scenic Trail, which leads eventually to the Florida Panhandle.

Turn right and proceed northeast on the dike, azimuth 25 degrees.

A large RV resort is on the left.

Tall casuarina trees now line the lake side of the dike; however, there are good views of the lake between gaps in the trees.

A small rim canal now parallels the dike on the left.

01.40 The dike swings to the east to an azimuth of 45 degrees.

A Florida National Scenic Trail campsite is adjacent to the lake. The view at this site is blocked by abundant Brazilian pepper trees that line the lake-front.

01.60 At this point, the view towards the lake is almost entirely blocked by dense growths of vegetation, including casuarina, Brazilian pepper, melaleuca, sabal palms, and other shrubbery.

01.90 The RV and trailer parks end and the area to the left, across the rim canal, is largely cattail marshland and cattle pasturage.

03.35 This point marks the west end of Jaycee Park and the end of the tree line that blocked the lake views. There is a great view of Lake Okeechobee from here.

04.00 Great views of the lake continue.

The rim canal is now densely lined with Brazilian pepper trees.

04.10 The dike begins to swing to the east, to an azimuth of 65 degrees.

Road to Jaycee Park.

At this point, the dike trail crosses the access road that leads into Jaycee Park.

End of Leg 20 and end of tour.

Bibliography

Brayfield, Lelia and William. *A Guide for Identifying Florida Fossil Shells and Other Invertebrates*, Gainesville, FL: Florida Paleontological Society, Inc., University of Florida, Third Edition 1993.

Brown, Robin C. *Florida's Fossils*, Sarasota, FL: Pineapple Press, Revised Edition 1996.

Burnett, Gene M. *Florida's Past, People and Events That Shaped the State*, Sarasota, FL: Pineapple Press, Volume 3, 1991.

Carmichael, Pete and Winston Williams. *Florida's Fabulous Reptiles & Amphibians*, Tampa, FL: World Publications, 1991.

Clark, Margaret Goff. *The Threatened Florida Black Bear*, New York, NY: Penguin Books, 1995.

Dasmann, Raymond F. *No Further Retreat, the Fight to Save Florida*, New York, NY: The Macmillan Co., 1971.

Douglas, Marjory Stoneman. *The Everglades: River of Grass, 50th Anniversary Edition*, Sarasota, FL: Pineapple Press, 1997.

George, Jean Craighead. *Everglades Wildguide*, Washington, D.C.: U.S. Government Printing Office, 1972.

Hanna, Alfred Jackson and Martha. *Lake Okeechobee, Wellspring of the Everglades*, Indianapolis, IN, Bobbs-Merrill Co., 1948.

Hoffmeister, John Edward. *Land from the Sea*, Miami, FL: University of Miami Press, 1974.

Lane, Ed. Special Publication No. 35, *Florida's Geological History and Geological Resources*, Tallahassee, FL: Florida Geological Survey, 1994.

McIver, Stuart B. *Dreamers, Schemers, and Scalawags, The Florida Chronicles, Volume I*, Sarasota, FL: Pineapple Press, 1994.

Morris, Allen and Joan Perry. *Florida Place Names*, Sarasota, FL: Pineapple Press, 1995.

National Geographic Society. *Field Guide to Birds of North America*, Second Edition, Washington, D.C.: National Geographic Society, 1987.

National Park Service. *Everglades, Official Map and Guide*, Washington, D.C.: U.S. Department of Interior, 1995.

Nelson, Gil. *The Trees of Florida*, Sarasota, FL: Pineapple Press, 1994.

Petuch, Edward J. *The Edge of the Fossil Sea*, Sanibel Island, FL: Bailey-Matthews Shell Museum, 1992.

Scott, Thomas M. *A Geological Overview of Florida*, Tallahassee, FL: Florida Geological Survey, 1992.

The Audubon Society. *Field Guide to North American Birds, Eastern Region*, New York, NY: Knopf, Inc., 1977.

Van Landingham, Kyle S. and Alma Hetherington. *History of Okeechobee County*, Orlando, FL: Daniels Publishers, 1978.

Walker, Steven L. and Matti P. Majorin. *Everglades, Wondrous River of Life*, Scottsdale, AZ: Elan Publishing, 1992.

White, William A. *Some Geomorphic Features of Central Peninsular Florida*, Tallahassee, FL: The Florida Geological Survey, 1958.

Will, Lawrence E. *A Cracker History of Lake Okeechobee*, St. Petersburg, FL: Great Outdoors Publishing Co., 1964.

Will, Lawrence E. *Okeechobee Catfishing*, St. Petersburg, FL: Great Outdoors Publishing Co., 1965.

Will, Lawrence E. *Okeechobee Hurricane, Killer Storms in the Everglades*, St. Petersburg, FL: Great Outdoors Publishing Co., 1967.

Will, Lawrence E. *Swamp to Sugar Bowl, Pioneer Days in Belle Glade*, St. Petersburg, FL: Great Outdoors Publishing Co., 1968.

Williams, Winston. *Florida's Fabulous Water Birds*, Tampa, FL: World Publications, 1983.

Index